THE ESSENCE OF
CHAOS

THE ESSENCE OF
CHAOS

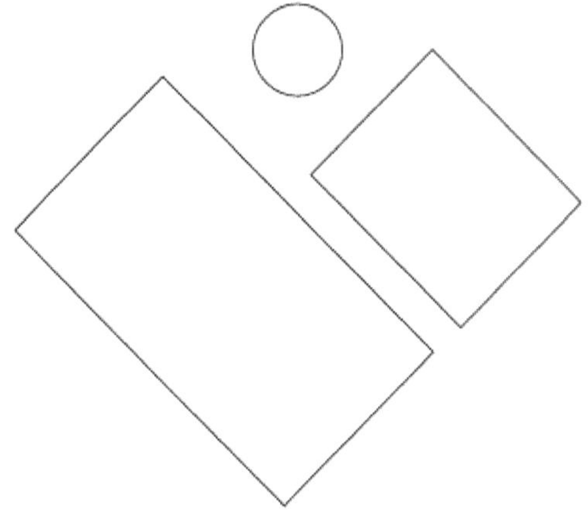

CREOZOE

An Ink Gladiators Press® Publication

Ink Gladiators Press®
Publishing and promoting warriors on life's battlefield

Ink Gladiators Press is an ePublishing company whose mission is to publish and promote writers, poets, lyricists, artists, and photographers through our current worldwide market distribution of over 3 billion readership. It is not affiliated with any other organization and is an independent ePublishing house. For Earthians who want to publish with us, check out our ongoing publishing opportunities on our Get Published page, or write to us to learn more about our professional Celestial Sky Services at the following email address: contact@inkgladiatorspress.com.

First Edition
Copyright © 2021 Timi Jolaoso (Creozoe)
The Essence Of Chaos

ISBN 13: 978-93-90766-34-5

Ink Gladiators Press®
Bangalore 560077, India
www.inkgladiatorspress.com

Credits:
Cover Art & Design - Creozoe
Developmental Editor - Reena Doss
Chief Copyeditor – Shruti Sharma
Book Design - Leonie Belle Hawk

To,

God, for the gift of creativity and family

Family, for the gift of love and friendship

Friends, for the gift of support in this world

World, for the gift of opportunities to be creative

Table Of Contents

1. Foreword...1

2. Introduction...2

3. Acknowledgments...165

4. Author's Note..167

5. Reviews...169

6. About The Author..170

7. Tell Us What You Think...171

Foreword

It gives me great pleasure to introduce The Essence of Chaos. Timi Jolaoso and I have known each other for 3 years and over time, I have read his poetry and seen it expand in depth. Timi is a talented and creative man, who designed the book cover logo for my poetry book Scattered Syllables. He is able to express his thoughts eloquently through both imagery and words.

Essentially, in my opinion, the essence of The Essence of Chaos is hope… and love.

Starting from the very first poem, it is clear that the words in this author's debut poetry book will take the reader on a healing journey. The Essence of Chaos, true to the title, contains poetry that showcases depth and complications of life. In some poems, Timi uses strength of character to overcome obstacles.

Timi Jolaoso's writing stylistically changes between his own original forms and known poetry styles, playing with words and rhyme. Some poems are musical, reading like song lyrics, such as XXI. There are a few poems within The Essence of Chaos which are short, containing good insight. Other pieces are longer, more imagery focused which leave the reader pondering.

There is a faith driven and thankfulness to God in Timi's poetry, highlighted in XLIII with the words, "God is love, Live with love."

I am proud of Timi Jolaoso that he has created The Essence of Chaos for his readers to enjoy.

Linda Lokhee @lindalokheeauthor

Author of
Scattered Syllables, Ink Quilled Thoughts,
The Night Noise and The Sock Monster

Introduction

...in the beginning God created the heavens and the earth... /

the earth was WITHOUT FORM and VOID /

in a state of CHAOS... /

Let the adventure begin... /

I

Faith to see brokenness as whole /

Is the treasure in forgiveness:
Surrender your defensiveness /

And embrace what you need to show:
"Letting go" is love's residence /
Faith to see brokenness as whole /

But /

This doesn't mean black is white as snow /
And you embrace deceptiveness /
Still, accept the effectiveness /

In the simple truth of having /
Faith to see brokenness as whole /

II

Beyond logic and reasoning /

What do you do when you have done /
All that you could have known, but run /

And fighting on is poisoning /
You find yourself always been shunned /
Beyond logic and reasoning /

But /

You're the only one listening /
Standing, facing a loaded gun /
Contemplating the rising sun /

Expecting something divine: God /
Beyond logic and reasoning /

III

Detach the past, take the lessons /

Write a new story everyday /
With every word you choose to say /

Prepare to fight for all seasons /
Ready to battle where you lay /
Detach the past, take the lessons /

And /

Decline sweet but lifeless reasons /
To keep your desires at bay /
Expand your territory; the Way /

To fight for the future today /
Detach the past, take the lessons /

IV

You would have been able to stand /

Your expectations were not him /
Love without commitment it seems /

Knowing it will never taste bland /
As long as it remains a dream /
You would have been able to stand /

But /

Your heart did fully understand /
Reality breaks at its seams /
When pressure collides with daydreams /

If you had embraced loneliness /
You would have been able to stand /

V

You are the warmth in the fire |

You are the peace in my storm |
The lines defining my form |

You are my only desire |
A fire that constantly burns |
You are the warmth in the fire |

You!

Protect me from all things dire |
Sprinkling divine to my norms |
Your words will always inspire |

A vehement burning for |
You are the warmth in the fire |

VI

Rain, Rain, Please don't go away |

Rain, Rain, soak me with showers |
For my seeds to bring flowers |

Ink flows from my pen this way |
Writing out that which devours |
Rain, Rain, Please don't go away |

See |

Changing seasons can be grey |
Yet, this love is always ours |
If you and I choose to stay |

Together, till we are old |
Rain, Rain, Please don't go away |

VII

I don't know how to be known /

It's a safe place, be open /
Yet, I cannot find my pen /

My heart is not yours to own /
So wait outside till it's ten /
I don't know how to be known /

But /

Do you know how to be known?
I cannot remember when /
You stopped acting like a clone /

Please can you leave me alone?
I don't know how to be known /

VIII

The silence in my DNA /

Can I stay with nothing to say /
And you and I will be okay?

Will your heart ultimately stray /
Into the worries of each day /
The silence in my DNA /

There!

In silence, you will find pure play /
If in stillness, we choose to lay /
Knowing your heart, I won't betray /

Can I show you where echoes sleep?
The silence in my DNA /

IX

Was it always this way?
This way is long, never ending /
Never ending is your love for me /
For me you said you would fight /
Would fight for you unconditionally /
You unconditionally chose me as yours /
As yours, I will always be /
Always be near me when I paint /
I paint of our love with the blood in my veins /
My veins pumped love songs from my heart /
My heart sings of the caress of my mind /
My mind is drowning in the love in you /
In you, I see the light /
The light where my love delights /
Love delights in the strength of your words /
Your words fuel my soul with might /
With might enough to take flight /
Take flight over stormy dark clouds /
Dark clouds thundering louder and louder /
And louder, my heart beats for you /
For you; anything I would do /
Would do you again and again /
And again, I see the light /
The light that makes love a delight /
A delight it is resting in the rain /
Resting in the rain without words to say /

X

I took pride for a ride /
Paid a price /
Shortening my rise /
Shutting my eyes to the truth that lies /
Beneath the love that dies /
Till my heart was cold as ice /

I tossed dice /
Looking for the draw /
To hide all things raw /
Shielding the wound from flies /

Light hides from me /
Screaming what am I to you?
A friend or a tool /
Your heart is cruel /

I found you in darkness /
You filled my heart with gladness /
My heart is tank full /
Of a love that pulls /
Me out of pride with a graceful stride /
Opening my eyes /
To the truth that lies /
Within a love filled with life /
I no longer have to strive /
Or see you as a tool /
For I am the thankful fool /

XI

Every morning, I wake /
My fragile hands, you take /

I know today, you'll make /
Something real out of fake /

For you took everything at stake /
On the cross for my sake /

Turning every mistake /
Into a glorious wake /

XII

No bleach! - life filled with colours /
A covenant without breach /
Yes reach! - Come close without fear /
The prince of peace is here to teach /

Preach! - Love sacrificed before life was created /
His faithfulness is never outdated /
As long as the waters come to kiss the shores /
Your mercy towards me is always sure /

Blend my mind with yours /
Your wisdom is sweeter than peaches /
Drown me in your presence /
Till I see my reflection in your eyes /

Each time I find myself resting in you /
I am undone, devoid of speech /

For you are the word in the beginning /
That determined my end with a beginning /
You are the voice in the end /
That said of my beginning with a glorious end /

XIII

Dethroned monster!
Where is your magic?
Dang! so tragic /
No strength left to muster /

A love potion /
A deadly notion /
Setting minds in motion /
Led to your demotion /

When the attractive /
Becomes the distracted /
The attracted /
Becomes the proactive /

The lust for a kingdom /
Turns a man into a dum-dum /
He is getting lost in his rum /
Someone spank his bum-bum /

Vain throats slashed with swords /
Liars bleed enchanting words /
Divinity not kept on guard /
Ends up being a facade /
Let me not be drunk in magic /
For that would be tragic /
To have all the powers in this world /
And yet be lacking in love /

XIV

Each careful caress causes my walls to swerve /
Etching memories of you in an endless verse /
Helplessly watching as my world hit reverse /

My starved spirit hungrily feeds /
Giving into your generous deeds /
Gentle hands planting new seeds /
Faith, hope, Love upon the soil /
Of my heart, my soul spoils /
For you, as I bask in the oils /
Of unconditional acceptance /
Embracing me at each instance /
Preventing me from losing my stance /

This love isn't perverse /
Eternally, it preserves /
Desires burning through my nerves /

XV

Distractions like an undine /
Beckons me to come and dine /
My soul has been famished /
Of carnal pleasures, I scream "damn it" /

8 months flying away from the bird cage /
Taking back what's left to salvage /
A journey towards serendipity /
Letting go of yesterday's self-pity /

My heart transforming into an amethyst /
I'm becoming stronger to say the least /
Breaking loose from that undead army /
With boisterous empty words so smarmy /
Blaring from trumpet - mouths like daffodils /
Shrilling to the ears with intentions to kill /

I rise above it all like a sanguine /
Not a wannabe, but genuine /
Walking drunk on authentic self-confidence wine /
Like I'm soaring on zephyr winds /
Stumbling upon beautiful finds /
The soul of beauty that binds /
My innermost being unwinds /
As her words rain strength on my soaked skin /
Making love to this divine being won't be a sin /
Her soft touch sends my mind into a spin /
Letting me know her heart is a win /

It's the voice of faith that speaks /
Sealing in my fate all that leaks /
Knowing well doubt is a killer /
Uncertainty, the sneaky mind-filler /
Yet in this love thriller /
My God is my pillar /
Thus, like a camera shutter /
My vision only taking pics that are sorta /
In line with my desires /
Only what you see should inspire /
Or what you don't see will snuff your fire /
Beckoning you to retire /

I know I have a strong oak chest /
Boldness brimming with zest /
The future is secure, I can rest /
Knowing I will counteract /
The things that try to retract /
My steps with the desire to attract /
Only what keeps me on track /

XVI

Sometimes being enough /
For yourself is enough /

It's the perfect little start /
To build something from the start /

Beauty is only a reflection /
Of how much you love your own reflection /

Try, try, try again till you get it right /
That's the pathway to all things right /

If you don't like something about yourself /
Embrace it, change it, recreate yourself /

Never give up on you /
There is only one you /

XVII

Absolute love, loves absolutely /
Fearless love, loves fearlessly /
Unconditional love, loves unconditionally /
Intentional love, loves intentionally /

Indifferent love, loves indifferently /
Careless love, loves carelessly /
Impatient love, loves impatiently /
A broken love, loves a broken way /

Love because you are /
Not because you need /

The strongest of hearts /
Belong to those who love /
Fearlessly... Intentionally... /
Unconditionally... Absolutely /

You cannot love like this /
If you haven't embraced /
God's love for you /

XVIII

Tell you the truth /
I will lie to you sometimes /
Because I know /
You won't handle the truth /
The way I want you to /

So /
Trust me /

XIX

Shape shifter /
Mindful drifter /
Time traveller /
Depth revealer /
Flying solo /
Taking it slow /
Keeping it low /
It's what I know /
It's my flow /
How I glow /
Your history /
Not my story /
Ain't no worry /
I ain't sorry /
Eyes ain't blurry /
I see His glory /

XX

Sometimes, I wonder /
Why you won't leave /

Sometimes, I wonder /
Why you never let me go /

Sometimes, I wonder /
Why you pursue still /

Sometimes, I wonder /
Why am I wondering /

XXI

Those voices in my head /
Those voices in my head /
Always reminding me why I bled /
Always reminding me why I bled /
Always reminding why I bled /
Those voices in my head /

The mouth that speaks reactively /
The mouth that speaks reactively /
Engages the heart in negativity /
Engages the heart in negativity /
The mouth that speaks negativity /
Engages the heart reactively /

My mentor told me to say nothing /
My mentor told me to say nothing /
In my heart to hide everything /
In my heart to hide everything /
My mentor told me to hide everything /
In my heart to say nothing /

Those voices in my head that speak reactively /
My mentor told me to say nothing /
Always reminding my head /
My mentor told me to hide everything /

Mentor, now I understand /
A man of loose lips /
Will always lose sleep /
For he drains himself of the strength to stand /

XXII

I'd rather walk alone into the sunset /
I'd rather walk alone into the sunset /
Than betray myself every sunrise /
Than betray myself every sunrise /
I'd rather walk alone into every sunrise /
Than betray myself into the sunset /

We would have made great lovers /
We would have made great lovers /
But we wanted to be just friends /
But we wanted to be just friends /
We would have been just friends /
But we wanted to be great lovers /

The odds were against us /
The odds were against us /
But our desires were for us /
But our desires were for us /
The odds were for us /
But our desires were against us /

I'd rather walk alone into the sunset as great lovers /
The odds were against us /
I'd rather walk alone as just friends /
But our desires were against us /

Now I understand friendship and love /
Is nothing but a decision to choose and be /
Knowing you could lose and see /
It doesn't mean two should fit like a glove /

XXIII

I hear you call my name /
I hear you call my name /
Child, come home, come home /
Child, come home, come home /
I hear you call: come home /
Child: Call my name /

Why would you desire me /
Why would you desire me /
I am not as pure as you are /
I am not as pure as you are /
Why would you; as you are /
I am not as pure; desire me /

Your love is divine /
Your love is divine /
But my mistake shines /
But my mistake shines /
Your love shines /
But my mistake is divine /

I hear you call my name; you desire me /
Your love is divine /
I hear you call as you are /
But my mistake is divine /

Nothing can separate us from the eternal /
No matter how many mistakes /
No matter how loud shame dictates /
His love will always be internal /

XXIV

Love is patient and kind /
Love is patient and kind /
Devotion is the fire that binds /
Devotion is the fire that binds /
Love is the fire that binds /
Devotion is patient and kind /

Love is not a feeling /
Love is not a feeling /
But the desire that is healing /
But the desire that is healing /
Love is desire that is healing /
But not a feeling /

Intentionality is the emotion of motion /
Intentionality is the emotion of motion /
Some wait for others to love them /
Some wait for others to love them /
Intentionality is to love them /
Some wait for the emotion of motion /

Love is patient and kind; not a feeling /
Intentionality is the emotion of motion /
Love is patient; love them /
Some wait for the emotion of motion /

Some say love is pain /
Others say it's better to find the right one /
However it doesn't matter if your heart is won /
By the one who doesn't see love as vain /

XXV

I believe in the purity of love /
I believe in the purity of love /
Even though I carry a broken heart /
Even though I carry a broken heart /
I believe I carry a broken heart /
Even though in the purity of love /

I am a hopeful romantic /
I am a hopeful romantic /
Yet my love is objective /
Yet my love is objective /
I am a hopeful: objective /
Yet my love is romantic /

Because His love pours in; spilling me out /
Because His love pours in; spilling me out /
Overflowing, covering you up /
Overflowing, covering you up /
Because His love pours, covering you up /
Overflowing, spilling me out /

I believe in the purity of love; a hopeful romantic /
Because His love pours in; spilling me out /
I believe in covering you up /
Overflowing, spilling me out /

To love anyone internally /
You need a source of love deeper /
A divine and eternal keeper /
In order to love them externally /

XXVI

I can see the battles in your heart /
I can see the battles in your heart /
You have lost the way to the start /
You have lost the way to the start /
I can see the way to the start /
You have lost the battles in your heart /

Just let go and trust me /
Just let go and trust me /
The journey is wild and crazy /
The journey is wild and crazy /
Just let's go wild and crazy /
The journey is to trust me /

You don't know where this path is going /
You don't know where this path is going /
But I see the beginning from the end /
But I see the beginning from the end /
You don't know the beginning from the end /
But I see where the path is going /

I can see the battles in your heart; trust me /
You don't know where this path is going /
I can see the battles from the end /
But I see where this path is going /

Trust God /
He alone knows where this goes /
The songs in all your woes /
He alone is good /

(This was written @ 2 /22 /21 @ 9:11 pm - Psalm 91:1)

XXVII

I know you feel like I have failed you /
I know you feel like I have failed you /
You trusted me to lead you /
You trusted me to lead you /
I know you trusted me /
Like I have to lead you /

All you see are walls /
All you see are walls /
The echoes of yesterday's calls /
The echoes of yesterday's calls /
All you see are yesterday's calls /
The echoes are walls /

And You wonder if I was leading you /
And You wonder if I was leading you /
Was it my voice you heard /
Was it my voice you heard /
And you wonder if you heard /
My voice was leading you /

I know you feel I have failed you: you see walls /
And you wonder if I was leading you /
I know you feel like it's my voice you heard /
My voice was leading you /

Just because you believed in something /
And it led you nowhere /
Or left you abandoned somewhere /
Doesn't mean it was nothing /

You believed – it's all that counts /
Believe some more...

XXVIII

To where you may question /
To where you may question /
It's not where I promised; you protest /
It's not where I promised; you protest /
To where I promised /
You may question; protest /

That which you wanted /
That which you wanted /
It is what I desired for you /
It is what I desired for you /
That which I desired for you /
It is what you wanted /

The timing was not right /
The timing was not right /
The parameters were incomplete /
The parameters were incomplete /
The timing was incomplete /
The parameters were not right /

To where you may question: you wanted /
The timing was not right /
To where: incomplete /
The parameters were not right /

Like a bird's view, He sees it all /
He knows the end from its beginning /
And the beginning from its end /
From our point of view; our heart only it all /

XXIX

So let go, so you don't lose the details /
So let go, so you don't lose the details /
I am the one in all of it /
I am the one in all of it /
So let go: all of it /
I am the one in the details /

Every step you take; I take with you /
Every step you take; I take with you /
Every move you make; I move with you /
Every move you make; I move with you /
Every step; I move with you /
Every move, I take with you /

So be brave, step out into the unknown /
So be brave, step out into the unknown /
You know, I will never let you go /
You know, I will never let you go /
So be brave, I will never let you go /
You, step out into the unknown /

So let go, so you don't lose the details I take with you /
So be brave, step out into the unknown /
So let go, I will never let you go /
You, step into the unknown /

I know it's difficult to let go /
And embrace uncertainty /
But remember His promises are certain /
That's all you need to know /

XXX

Trust me, let go /
Trust me, let go /
How?! I hear you whisper /
How?! I hear you whisper /
Trust me, I hear you whisper /
How? Let go /

How do I let go of a dream I longed for?
How do I let go of a dream I longed for?
Do I stop expecting your promises?
Do I stop expecting your promises?
How do I let go of your promises?
Do I stop expecting a dream?

Let your eyes be fixed on me /
Let your eyes be fixed on me /
For I am your promises fulfilled /
For I am your promises fulfilled /
Let your eyes be fulfilled /
For I am your promises fixed on me /

Trust me, let go of a dream longed for /
Let your eyes be fixed on me /
Trust me, I am your promises fulfilled /
For I am your promises fixed on me /

There is nothing else to be said /
It's a choice to start anew /
Knowing He makes all things new /
It's the price He paid /

XXXI

The realm beyond logic /
Where reasoning suffocates /
The crucible where blind hope is forged /
And radical faith becomes the mind of a man /

A warrior must know this /
"When a man is passive, generations suffer" /
He must not spend his time chasing beauty /
For her depths, logic and reasoning cannot define /

A warrior must stoke the fire of love /
And fan the flame of faith /
Forging a hope that is blinded to this world /
Yet alive to the things of God /

Or he will waste this strength /
On strangers from unknown lands /
Coming into the worst type of poverty /
The poverty of the spirit /

When the battles of life come /
He will have no strength to fight /
Becoming the prisoner of thieves /
Robbing him of what's left - his vision /

Dear warrior /
Block your ears with the word of God /
That you may not be swayed by the doctrines of men /
Who have become passive in heart /

Ask them to wage war /
And see how they will soar /
They speak of taking a city /
While their homes are in ruins /

They go around warring against active women /
To protect a throne, claiming it's their created right /
If then it is your birthright /
Why strip her down in order to sit on it?

I do not speak as a man /
Who has all things figured out /
I only speak as a man /
Who knows his deepest battles must be won /

For beauty desires to be fought for /
She will not submit to passive men /
Men who are distracted by her presence /
Men who see her as the ultimate goal in life /

But then, there is beauty locked up /
On the inside of every man /
Crying out day and night to be set free /
Yet she will not submit to /
The passivity of her host either /
For he is not her ultimate goal /

The ultimate goal of beauty /
Is divine expression in three forms /
Faith, Hope, Love /

For the man who fights for /
His own inner beauty to radiate /
Is the active man /
The man who has no reason to defend a throne /
For he has made Faith, Hope, Love his home /

So yes /
I do not listen to men who are deaf to what's important /
My ears are locked on the most important to me /

The author and perfecter of Faith, Hope, Love /
Jesus /

XXXII

Desire cannot be negotiated /
Yet I was taught she needs to be initiated /
Something I am unlearning /
Decluttering my discerning /
For love becomes contracted /
When she isn't attracted /

Losing traction to a passive attraction /
Is to suffer deliberate self-inflicted infractions /
Embracing active distractions /

The medium is the message /
Unrequited love is a worthless massage /
Desire should not require an initiation /
Love is not a negotiation /

XXXIII

When your tongue turns into a dagger /
Because your actions turn her into a nagger /
When you slash her back with lashes /
Because your rage shouldn't burn you to ashes /
When your words became incisions /
Because you couldn't make painful decisions /
To dig up the lies you watered like rain /
Your pursuit of an ego leading you in vain /
You wanted her desires for you to get waned /
So you could call her stained /
It's not you, it's her - the game /
Irritation was the cane /
To beat her mercilessly until she caved /
To the path your silly mind paved /
She is stubborn - she is to blame /
She won't yield - so you quench her flame /

She gave herself to you - which was lame /
A truth you will never muster up the courage to blame /

XXXIV

What can I go without?

I can go without the type of love that words describe /
Only actions write memories like a poetic scribe /

When the silence of life embraces my heart /
Like a leech sucking up the air in my lungs /
And I no longer recollect where I belong /

When we share each molecule of oxygen like it's...
Our last...
Those are the moments when faces drift away /
And I'm left... all curled up at the corner of my own darkness /
Drowning in the pool of my own tears... remembering words /
That were spoken of a love that couldn't find a moment to...
Breathe life into me...

A love that is so scared of darkness that it wouldn't find /
The courage to be my light /
A love that is nothing but an idea devoid of intentionality /
A love that is nothing but a good idea with a bad penalty /
A love that is nothing but an excuse for a soul's brutality /
A love that ignores its own abilities to create possibilities /
Screaming louder on the streets that it's my responsibility /

A love so quick to promise to suck it up /
But so quick to compromise and lock it up /

They say I have a lone wolf mentality /
It's because spoken love left /
When I was faced with a bad reality /
Trading my desires to fulfill your desires /
Forgetting that is what makes us all expire /

For love is the energy we need when things fall apart /
To start all over again, healing all broken parts /

Love is the light that should unzip our darkness |
Love is the only component that never fails |

The love that fails, that which words give life to...
That love I can go without |

For when we are all out of words, what is left?

XXXV

Images of the past you wish you can't remember |
Flashes of that day you wish never came |
You wonder if he ever bothered |
Your feathers couldn't stand that stormy weather |

Hmmm!

You remember that day, just like yesterday |
It was for a second, you took your eyes off him |
You wonder if he ever beckoned |
For you not to look the other way |

Hmmm!

He said he will never let go |
That's all you needed to know |
He said it's gonna turn out okay |
Because for you he will make a way |

Hmmm!

Broken wings are all I'm seeing |
Yet forever you call me into being |
My love, your love is so forgiving |
I never really understand what you are thinking |

Hmmm!

Yet again, I will trust you |
Cos you always help me to burst through |
Realities that are not true |
Situations that are not new |

So I will pick up my broken wings and fly away |
On my knees, I'll choose to pray |
Even when things are difficult to say |
You never keep me at bay |

Yeah!

You always have my back /
No wonder I have nothing to lack /
Even when all seems so stormy and dark /
You always hide me in your ark /

So Imma flap my broken wings /
With the joy that Your love brings /
You are all I got so am clinging /
I am all You bought, so I'm singing /

Because /
Broken wings still fly /
It's Your love we have /
Broken wings still fly /
It's Your life You gave /
Broken wings still fly /
It's Your joy, we laugh /
Broken wings still fly /
It's Your grace, we live

His blood flows through your veins /
In your heart He reigns /
Your broken wings aren't in vain /
He is healing your pain /

So today we trust Him with /
Those who broke us /
Those who mocked us /
Those who locked us /
Dreams that never came true /
Cos they all have broken wings /

Broken wings still fly /

XXXVI

You kiss my heart with your affections /
Lost for words: how can I show my appreciation /
All I have, I give you in complete devotion /
Worshipping you with all of my emotions /

There is a type of fondness /
That grows in a simple friendship /
It's way deeper than infatuations /
It's a fire that burns every drop of lust /

You are my magnificent passion /
Everything you are, I totally respect /
Your hold is tough, your touch tender /
The fibres of my being surrender in adulation /

You can call it an obsessive attachment /
The buds on my tongue find you delightful /
You can call it an addictive enchantment /
I'll keep eating you till I am full /

Burning in your flame /
Apart from your presence, what else is there to relish /
In your heart, I have found a soft spot /
My beloved, my love is real: not a sport /

XXXVII

When things tear /
You are here /
When things cause tears /
Your heart always hears /
My unexpressed troubles /
You hug me in doubles /
Keeps me humble /
Causing my heart to tumble /
Covering me when I fumble /
I have no need to grumble /
When my stomach rumbles /

Your love is eternal /
You fill up my internal /
With joy and laughter /
My battle cry starter /
You are my Maker /
You are my life's partaker /
My worst fear /
Is never near /
For You always bear /
My every tear and wear /

XXXVIII

Buried in a place unknown /
Is the man once known /

XXXIX

I am not trying to be right /
It's useless, really useless /
I am okay being real /
It's messy, really messy /
Being right is easy, really easy /
Embrace your ideals long enough /
Being real is hard, really hard /
Be truthful for a day /
Shock the world with what you say /

Soon you will find out /
There is no right way to anything /
But the way of truth /
That is what sets you free /
From the shackles of the ideal /

XL

Strung my bow /
I won't take a bow /
I am Yours now /
All I need to know /

You won't take flight /
For You I will fight /
In You I have found light /
Making my heart light /

I will wait every night /
For You are my might /
You found me by twilight /
Your countenance so bright /

When all seems low /
And I have lost my flow /
When all seems slow /
And I have lost my glow /

Still nothing separates me from You /
Still You move everything to whisper "I love you" /

XLI

It's that feeling of infatuation /
When I find myself in this situation /
Expressing my heart in sacred devotion /
Giving voice to every emotion /

When I find myself in this situation /
Words aren't enough for communication /
I wrap myself in the sounds of appreciation /
Divine, beyond my mind's comprehension /

Words aren't enough for communication /
Let me drown in a pool of endless adulation /
Not for love's recommendation /
But for my beloved's adoration /

Let me drown in a pool of endless adulation /
This isn't an attempt to recreate flirtation /
For I am caught up in a fixation /
This is my ultimate elevation /

This isn't an attempt to recreate flirtation /
For that would be to worship creation /
Which has a fixed duration /
Propped up by a shaky foundation /

For that would be to worship creation /
A recipe for my soul's dehydration /
The poisonous sensation /
That results in an everlasting sedation /

A recipe for my soul's dehydration /
It's that feeling of infatuation /
The poisonous sensation /
Expressing my heart in sacred devotion /

XLII

Love never failed /
Innocent hands nailed /
Death - stained tales /
Freedom always trailed /

Innocent hand nailed /
Guilty hands raised /
Bloodstained veils /
Freedom from jails /

Guilty hands raised /
His back bruised /
Faith, religion derailed /
The law, reclaimed /

His back bruised /
Love was crushed /
Souls were washed /
Our mistakes squashed /

Love was crushed /
Condemnation; hushed /
Restoration; rushed /
Sin is flushed /

Condemnation; hushed /
Love is a must /
Truth you can trust /
Dust off the dust /

Love is a must /
Love never failed /
Truth, you can trust /
Death - stained tales /

XLIII

You are love /
Created to love /
God is love /
Live with love /

Created to love /
By giving love /
In receiving love /
For sharing love /

By giving love /
Enter into love /
By discovering love /
You know love /

Enter into love /
Trusting in love /
Believing in love /
Unafraid of love /

Trusting in love /
Freely embracing love /
Listening to love /
Observing love /

Freely embracing love /
Love into love /
Being with love /
Built for love /

Love into love /
You are love /
Being with love /
God is love /

XLIV

I hated everything you stood for /
Deep down within my core /
Even your beauty is abhorred /
The idea of being with you; absurd /

Deep down within my core /
I reacted to the pride you wore /
Arrogance dripping from your sweat pore /
Stains a dirty floor /

I reacted to the pride you wore /
When you spoke like an asshole /
Displaying grandiosity like a décor /
Confidence becoming an eyesore /

When you spoke like an asshole /
I shut the door; watched from a peephole /
Asking myself if this is all /
I get it, you have accomplished all /

I closed the door; watched from a peephole /
Asked myself whose attention you stole /
Lonely; sleeping on a cold floor /
Wondering why you are being ignored /

Asked myself whose attention you stole /
From making yourself swole /
Inflated with pride; a big bore /
A tasteless wine; you'd pour /

From making yourself swole /
I hated everything you stood for /
Inflated with pride; a big bore /
Even your beauty is abhorred /

XLV

You might be wondering who was that for /
To be honest, it's the insecurity I stole from /
I could have loved you like I thought of /
But the sweetest wine, I yearned for /

To be honest, it's the insecurity I stole from /
When people let themselves be misinformed /
There is hidden beauty in all things unformed /
If and only if we let our hearts be formed /

When people let themselves be misinformed /
By past bruises, they let their lives be formed /
In such a way that everyone is meant to conform /
To whatever ideals their minds form /

By past bruises, they let their lives be formed /
By letting go of the desires to be transformed /
While wondering why no pursuit is performed /
When the perspective of love is deformed /

By letting go of the desires to be transformed /
How can healthy love be spurned /
You said your trust should be earned /
When your duplicity is confirmed /

How can healthy love be spurned /
When it's all according to your terms /
When I decided to keep my sperms /
"Insecure" is the label I earned /

When it's all according to your terms /
You might be wondering who was that for /
When I decided to keep my sperms /
I could have loved you like I thought of /

XLVI

I know what you are thinking /
What am I drinking?
Spewing out words that are stinking /
Without even blinking /

What am I drinking?
Memories that I am unthinking /
Broken bells rusting /
Ringing melodies whispering /

Memories that I am unthinking /
From my foolishness now clicking /
Truth preventing me from swinging /
From mercy to limping /

From my foolishness now clicking /
I am faced with a harsh new beginning /
The message is now convincing /
It was my fault - letting it sink in /

I am faced with a harsh new beginning /
I was never a good guy - but a wildling /
Never was I good at arse licking /
I'd rather be sprinting than clinging /

I was never a good guy - but a wildling /
You can blame it on my upbringing /
My truest nature is constantly ringing /
Untamed love is what I am bringing /

You can blame it on my upbringing /
I know what you are thinking /
My truest nature is constantly ringing /
Spewing out words that are stinking /

XLVII

I beseech thee /
Do not cozen thyself /
For thou hath a beautiful soul /
We ought not forget thou art a gift /

Do not cozen thyself /
Thou lifts souls caught in a drift /
Verily thou art not perfect /
Yet, I cannot consider you a defect /

Thou lifts souls caught in a drift /
For thy presence causes a shift /
So pleasant and swift /
Changing gears like a short-shift /

For thy presence causes a shift /
I am forever entangled in this love twist /
Awaiting the next time we... kiss /
Filling the bathroom with mist /

I am forever entangled in this love twist /
Thou hath the damsel I wished /
Who you are is described in my list /
Your kindness I cannot resist /

Thou hath the damsel I wished /
A dream I didn't know existed /
Yet, I pleaded with God to shortlist /
This eternal stock list /

A dream I didn't know existed /
I beseech thee /
Yet, I pleaded with God to shortlist /
For thou hath a beautiful soul /

XLVIII

My heart is broken /
By words that were spoken /
I wonder if pain is love's token /
For my hope is stolen /

By words that were spoken /
My dreams were frozen /
Drained of the faith for motion /
Maybe love is just an ancient notion /

My dreams were frozen /
God, will I ever get chosen?
For time is speedily closing /
With no hope it might reopen /

God, will I ever get chosen?
By love as deep as the ocean /
That is what I am hoping /
Or I am drunk in fantasy's love potion /

By love deep as the ocean /
Like a dry skin to a moisturizing lotion /
Soothing my heart with a faith golden /
In your presence, you'll find me soaking /

Like a dry skin to a moisturizing lotion /
Let my heart be free and open /
By hope that is always hoping /
Knowing your plans for me are provoking /

Let my heart be free and open /
My heart is broken /
By hope that is always hoping /
I wonder if pain is love's token /

XLIX

Tap into the pain within /
There you'll find where to begin /
Give yourself time to re-think /
If and only if you are making a plan /

There you'll find where to begin /
After you discover your original sin /
"You cannot know how to handle everything" /
If you haven't previously encountered some things /

After you discover your original sin /
Find a way to conquer that thing /
That led you to everything /
That was actually nothing /

Find a way to conquer that thing /
You know the pleasure it brings /
Is nothing but a fling that stings /
Leaving you with broken wings /

You know the pleasure it brings /
You know the songs it sings /
Isn't worship to the one true king /
Yet tugs on your apron strings /

You know the songs it sings /
You know the sounds of its strings /
You know you should play the thing /
Re-digging your wellsprings /

You know the sounds of its strings /
Tap into the pain within /
You know you should play the thing /
Give yourself time to rethink /

L

To trust you with all my heart /
To walk the hardest paths /
To call my scars divine art /
Is all you have asked /

To walk the hardest paths /
To discover beautiful starts /
To face my darkest past /
Is all you have asked /

To discover beautiful starts /
To let go of dreams passed /
To discover opportunities vast /
Is all you have asked /

To let go of dreams passed /
To recover from a heart crushed /
To be quiet while getting lashed /
Is all you have asked /

To recover from a heart crushed /
To be patient while being rushed /
To embrace being trashed /
Is all you have asked /

To be patient while being rushed /
To choose love while feeling lust /
To ignore all things unjust /
Is all you have asked /

To choose love while feeling lust /
To trust you with all of my heart /
To ignore all things unjust /
To call my scars divine art /

LI

Love is patient and kind /
The best gift you can find /
If you are willing to be blind /
To the imperfections of the mind /

The best gift you can find /
The love that is mined /
Beneath the fears of the mind /
Throwing insecurities to the wind /

The love that is mined /
The love that is mine /
To be eternally entwined /
In a love that is divine /

The love that is mine /
With blood was signed /
Forever accepted, not denied /
Never abandoned on the wayside /

With blood was signed /
All troubles spoken with a sigh /
Thus my soul will rise high /
No longer shall love hide /

All troubles spoken with a sigh /
To all memories that ended in a cry /
While drowning in a sea of whys /
Yet, there is a reason to look into the sky /

To all memories that ended in a cry /
Love is patient and kind /
While drowning in a sea of whys /
If you are willing to be blind /

LII

Dear future wife /

I cannot make you promises /
You cannot protect me from your hisses /
When life serves us with near misses /
I can only smear you with many kisses /

You cannot protect me from your hisses /
In times you feel I don't deserve your kisses /
For life doesn't always favour good intentions /
It's okay to serve me with your contentions /

In times you feel I don't deserve your kisses /
Always remember why you are my Mrs /
For I have acknowledged life isn't a fairy-tale /
Broken promises make a lover's heart stale /

Always remember why you are my Mrs /
My helpmate when my strength misses /
What makes our lives the perfect tale /
When we walk down uncertain trails /

My helpmate when my strength misses /
My life partner until my heart seizes /
To pump the life that creates connections /
And gives purpose directions /

My life partner until my heart seizes /
Until my body freezes /
Until I lie there: pale /
Because my soul has sailed /

Until my body freezes /
I cannot make you promises /
Until I lie there: pale /
When life serves us with near misses /

LIII

She said I was too mysterious /
I wondered if she was serious /
Maybe playfully curious /
Or thinks I am an idiot /

I wondered if she was serious /
Cos some are simply devious /

Occasionally wearing a red blouse /
Speaking words quite delirious /

Cos some are simply devious /
Curious about what isn't obvious /
Relax, "there will never be an us" /
You ain't riding my big bus /

Curious about what isn't obvious /
Attention seeking quite nefarious /
Leading you on into something notorious /
An entanglement quite insidious /

Attention seeking quite nefarious /
As she could be supercilious /
Wearing a countenance hideous /
Yet expressing beauty: quite lascivious /

As she could be supercilious /
Her company was delicious /
So, I decided to be un-seriously serious /
Something that makes her furious /

Her company was delicious /
She said I was too mysterious /
So, I decided to be un-seriously serious /
Maybe playfully curious /

LIV

Sometimes when I fart /
I redirect the fragrance /
To my nose /

Just to remind myself of /
How much of a BADASS /
I am /

LV

I write /
Because paper doesn't talk back /
It stares blank /
Soaking in all the ink /
Keeping it in /
Dutifully reserving its judgements /
Loving, reserving its arguments /
It's got no narratives /
Never gives me ratings /

LVI

Go home to your wife /
Or meet with the knife /
In the hands of the hot chocolate /
Stranger who invites you on a date /
That seduces your mind late /
In the night /

Her words promise euphoric heights / /
Hiding poisonous bites
"Relax, it's only a glass of champagne" /
So begins her dangerous campaign /

LVII

I'd say I love you /
But /
I'd have to find out first /

LVIII

Gave me /
But you would rather /
Crave me /

Be brave /
Enough to come closer /
Have me /

LIX

It's that feeling when...
You no longer care if you are liked /
It's a different kind of freedom /

LX

Most of them are not that strong /
Only masters in the art of hiding self /
And exposing others /

52

LXI

You are all I want /
You are all I ever need /
Nothing else satisfies me /

Without You, no me /
Within You, I find purpose /
I have love, I need nothing else /

LXII

We search for unconditional acceptance /
By putting conditions on those giving it /

A warrior must learn to accept himself unconditionally /
Ridding himself completely of the conditions others impose /

LVXIII

Get lost in /
The depths of me /
Let me explore /
The universe of you /
We shall create a multi-verse /
Uniquely diversely /
Us /

LXIV

She was enveloped /
By love developed /
During the harsh winter colds:
A warm heart that never folds /

LXV

Why should I exploit you, my love?
When there is so much more about God's goodness to explore /

LXVI

Body tattooed all over by fingerprints /
From a love branded by fire /

LXVII

Took her to that place where /
Roses sweat on petals /
Tears words couldn't let out /

Trapped in an embrace of practical devotion /
Sunk deep in mysteries /

She wanna know things she'll never know /

LXVIII

You invade my time zone with you /
Without leaving room for me to say no /
Cos you know it doesn't matter /
You are you and I love it /

LXIX

Who am I?

A trans-dimensional powerful spirit /
With a soul and body, capable of creating /
Everything out of nothing /

LX

To search for love in the wrong places /
Is to find love outside of God /
For God is love /

LXI

I have heard it said /
Prayer doesn't change all things /

"It's because you haven't prayed long enough" /

For prayer changes you first /
Before all things /

LXII

I don't know how to be known /
Or if I should belong /
I do know how to be me /
That should be enough /

LXIII

Self-help without God's help leads to helplessness /

For what do you do in seasons beyond the realm of logic /
And reasoning /

LXIV

I have been through many things /
The silent screams my heart sings /
The pains even though still stings /
Cannot be compared to the joy hope brings /

Let go of the past /
The process is slow, not that fast /
For every day, I still see the whole cast /
Reminding me of forgiveness, at the start /

Forgiveness isn't letting go of the lessons they taught /
For that is how my gullible innocence brought forth /
Weapons for the future that is wrought /
In the pains of the past, I never sought /

LXV

We celebrate /
Not when we liberate /
The not so brief pain experiencing relief /
You gotta keep glowing /
In the midst of all you keep from showing /
Cos the attitude of gratitude increases your altitude /
Setting your goals higher than the sun /
Pursuing with vehemence all things that turn you on /
The friend that holds your hands till the end /
Creating deep laughter in the midst of all that falters /

Sometimes the greatest songs are not always melodious /
Sometimes they are songs of hope while enduring /
Something odious /
Even lovemaking in all its bliss creates steamy hisses /
If love was without pain /
How would we measure its gain /
Baby please, it's too late now to give your heart on a lease /

LXVI

A detachment from past disappointment /
Attaches you to present realities /
Thus preparing you /
To fight for what you desire the most /
For it's better to fight and be uncomfortable /
Than walk the road with each step reminding you /
Of a future that never came /
Desires that never became realities /

LXVII

Detach from the past /
Take the lessons /
Detach from the faces /

Stay connected to today /
Fight for today /
Write a different story /
Expand your territory /
Confront your fears with creativity /

Prepare for the future /
The future is tomorrow /
Prepare to fight /
For tomorrow is yesterday's today /

LXVIII

I think it's a good thing /
I don't want it to stop /

I want you all to myself /
Sharing you with the world too /

You are my story /
You are the best thing in me /

You are my utmost desire /
You are all I could ever have /

LXIX

How do I get through the darkness?!

It's simple!

My eyes are forever stuck on Him /

He is my light /
Like a moon to a sun /
I reflect His light to my darkness /

LXX

You fed me with your quixotic passion /
Saying it should be my ideal vision /
You said it would be like catching stars /
All my heart caught were swift darts /
Exploring your tormenting labyrinth /
Of promises like counterfeit fingerprints /
Etched upon my skin in silvered moments /
Of unbearable cyclic torments /
Even the sweetness of zephyr winds /
Cannot soothe this bondage that binds /

You forget that I am ya amar /
Truth that can only be seen from afar /
For my once well-watered garden now xeric meadows /
Because of your sacred hollow vows /
I would have preferred you forgot me in the woodlands /
Perhaps I would have been able to stand /
But you left me hanging by a thread /
From a steep edge that screams dread /

Your heart hides a vexatious tyranny /
Your smiles expressing eternal chivalry /
Drawing another into your universe of the underworld /
Stripping her of everything that spells bold /
She falls into your tribulations of eternity /
As you slowly scrape off her identity /
Your intentions, a sardonic revenge /
Leaving another body with no one to avenge /

Yet I burn to crisp the jealousy of the dragon /
Stopping its torments from dragging on /
Finding protection under iridescent wings /
The camouflage of colours it brings /

My feathers flutter sounding like harmonious thunders /
Masking out the noise of my past blunders /
As I beheaded giants and goblins /
Dumping what's left of them in hellish bins /
To be lost /forgotten in faded moments /
Cherishing even my slowest movements /
As I explore these echoless shores /
Giving the whole of me into its lures /

I stand face to face with my divine messenger /
Speaking the words "welcome ruthless passenger" /

LXXI

The change is constant /
Something new every instant /
Like a rapture of the deep /
Taking all which is asleep /
Transforming me into a questing beast /
Hunting for treasures for a feast /
I have a prophecy of hope /
That causes me to elope /
From that odious fiend /
Vying for my untimely end /
Thus, I relish sweet nectars of knowledge /
Over him, I always have an edge /
Keeping me away from meandering delusions /
Alerting me of glittering slithering inclusions /
That great, yet powerless leviathan of my soul /
The resistance that always screams foul /
Towards my heart's kindred whispers /
With the aim of creating dream blisters /

LXXII

The sirens can't get me now /
Sweet voices asking for a bow /
Broken souls craving attention /
Deeply entangled in tension /
They all got a block /
Saving me my luck /
My mind flushes out their images /
Leaving no damages /
Keep your eyes straight /
On the vision so great /
Look not right or left /
Forgetting the past you felt /
My eyes on one single price /
Ghosts won't roll my dice /
Each morning I rise /
Constantly building my enterprise /

LXXIII

We hold on to past crimes /
Choking up our hearts with grime /
We get scared of love at times /
Especially when it's in its prime /

We forget love takes time /
For it grows in full-time /
Sometimes we want half-time /
Especially when our soul craves downtime /

If your love could only be a mime /
Would your words need to chime /
Should it be a new paradigm /
If your love becomes a pantomime /

I understand this is springtime /
And you are pressed for time /
I know you don't want love sublime /
But pressure creates sweet wine /

LXXIV

The salted air that is tasteless /
The aimless meander that is wasteful /
If I could suck out the waters from damped leaves /
My rants would not be louder than crying gulls /

Yet, I find myself drifting along the rivers of life /
Wearing my least favourite hat /
In a tar-patched raft (my heart) /
Hoping to stray from strife /

The morning air is the sign of a new day /
The hope that someday our love will be like opening buds /
Until we keep looking to the moon, heavily ladened /
Wearing dusty shoes from walking along the dunes of life /
Hoping to find green grass at some point /

Perhaps, I should escape into the fields of flowers /
Wandering along the paths to find what empowers /
While listening intently to nature's playlists /
Bumblebee wings buzzing in tune to artificial beats /

Yet again I find myself on an untested trail /
The thoughts of breaking them in tells me I'm frail /
Perhaps I smoked a wild mushroom /
Getting lost in purple dreams, hoping to drown what looms /

Perhaps, I bask in sun-brushed drifting memories /
Letting go of the desires for vain glories /
That one day I may slip off a ridge line into a high mountain lake /
Embarrassed like a wet dog, yet boldness I had to fake /
Forgetting I intentionally crossed the yellow lines /
Ignoring the cries of the rambling roads for that which blinds /

Perhaps at last we discover /
We have become strong like cedar /
Saturated with shades and hues /
Filled with splinter scars from pine barks /

Or maybe we only remember /
How we have been burned to crisp /
While singing the blues /
Becoming other people's unwanted bites /

LXXV

I am nothing but a broken man /
Looking at life from a broken view /

I do not need you to fix me /
Your views are broken too /

Is it healing if the pieces are glued together?!
I can still see the cracks in your words /

Is it healing when I give you what's unbroken in me /
In exchange for what's unbroken in you /

Even that takes a different kind of healing /
For we fear we might just break that too /

So, give me what's already broken /
Let me love the pieces as a whole /

Reserve what's unbroken to yourself /
Only you can keep it whole /

LXXVI

It's the ebb and flow /
The high and low /
That make us glow /

You need to know /
The sun will show /
The wind will blow /

Time may be slow /
You may fail at your role /
In need of a tow /

Like the sun, show /
Like the wind, blow /
Make yourself scream: WOW /

For it's the mind's surprise /
That gives the courage to rise /
Walking firmly on ice /
Reaching for the stars /

LXXVII

A heart of compassion /
Always calls for action /
It's never reactive /
But always proactive /

Be bold, stand up for those who cannot speak /
Be fearless, even when others want to sneak /

You can be everything you want to be /
Whatever that may be, requires that you see /
You've got everything you need /
The power within, you should wield /

Love is where hard work meets perseverance /
The battle to be great is your only deliverance /

LXXVIII

Good people are rarely perfect /
Neither should you embrace a project /
Someone who has neglected his or her defects /
By viewing you as various objects /

A cure for an itch /
A thread for a stitch /
A fix for a glitch /
A tool for a hitch /

Everyone is required to respond to an ability within /
Should you have to account for their abilities to begin? /
If they disagree with their abilities within /
Should you be the cure to begin? /

Good people are rarely perfect /
Good people have defects /
If love was the subject /
No one should be viewed as objects /

LXXIX

The dreams that stream /
From my subconscious /
Leave me unconscious /
It seems my possibilities /
Are deemed impossibilities /
Perhaps my stem isn't strong enough /
I find myself wanting to be stern /
In order to make a turnover of benefits /
Regardless of where my point of origin is /
In relation to their framework /
Yet I know, the only way /
To discover who I really am /
Is to embrace, brace for impact /
Running the race in extremes /
Knowing I have to break pacts /
With or without tact /
Ditching the class act /

LXXX

Fickle, fickle little heart /
How I wonder what lies beneath /
Broken words, dreams, ended forevers /
Promises made, yet never met /
Fickle, fickle little heart /
How I wonder what lies beneath /

When the bound angels are free /
When the broken sky within is gone /
Then your words will be whole, full of light /
And your promises fulfilled /
Fickle, fickle, little heart /
How I wonder when you will be healed /

LXXXI

Desperation caught me in a cuckold /
Hopefully I don't end up cold /
It's hard to pull the cords on my dreams /
Accepting everything else that streams /
I tell my mind it's not what it seems /
I told my heart not to release its steams /
Today reminds me of my past /
The part I left to last /
For I had but a shelter /
To protect me from my heart's stormy weather /

When your heart is overrun /
In a selfless pursuit that overturns /
When you have had it /
And you no longer want to have it /
When you can't trust anyone again /
And you have labor for turns in vain /
When you wonder how you lost your place /
And realize you never had it in the first place /
When you realize you created a wrong narrative /
In order to keep false faces attractive /

Tonight, I return to my shelter /
Embracing its silence /
This time, my guts I won't ignore /
For cracked isn't my lens /
Little before me is this fence /
No longer will I go where I don't want to go /
No longer will I be less of myself for anyone /
No longer will I give up my grounding /
No matter how right it's sounding /
It will always be my frame /
You can hold on to your shame /
You will no longer be my blame /
Tonight, I reignite my flame /

LXXXII

I remember the season of fame /
Everywhere I went, I heard my name /
But then I remember the scandals /
That took off my sandals /
Walking barefoot upon the lies /
Looking into the eyes of trust as she dies /
They formed narratives /
To fuel selfish imperatives /

Today my heart is cold /
I seek no one to hold /
I don't wanna be that close /
I am tired of such a dose /

These days I listen with my eyes /
Watching what may suffice /
Burning cold like ice /
Letting patience be my vice /

LXXXIII

Masquerades in a parade /
Playing charades in an arcade /
Pop culture is a masque whose task /
Is to keep truth welded to a mask /
Yet no matter how we hide what's on the inside /
Our mouths spew covertly to the outside /
The hunger for acceptance is louder on the streets /
Than the lies of freedom our hearts entreat /
Yet we seek the face of love to behold our mold /
Freedom we bemoan /
Forgetting the hidden mystery of freedom /
Is to love in wisdom /
Yet wisdom is devoid of a mask /
If you ask /

LXXXIV

Shame has a language /
The language of superiority /
Shame has an emotion /
The emotion of inferiority /

Who made you feel ashamed of your desires?! /
Those whom your ideas don't inspire /
Remember you are your own emperor /
Failing to go after your desire is your own error /

LXXXV

How do we know if it's discernment or fear /
If we don't take that step and come near /
I am not seeking the perfect how /
If it takes away the place of honesty now /
Some say if I continue this way, I will keep losing out /
To be one with God, myself and others, is what I am about /
After all, He died on the cross for me to be whole /
Pretence shouldn't be something I should know /

LXXXVI

They say it's a numbers game /
I wonder how many before you came /
Would I have anything left to share?
Would you have any strength left to bear?
If comparison is the reason /
To go through the season /
Guess we will never learn the lesson /
You will never be the ideal person /
For there is always better /
Eventually you will cease to matter /
Even the luckiest of draws /
Is steeped in so many flaws /
No wonder we are all players /
Savage scavenging slayers /
For really if it's a numbers game /
There are many broken hearts before you came /
Why should yours or mine be an exception?
Distrust should be the inception /
You deserve no exemption /
Let's enjoy this fleeting temptation /

Why don't you agree?
It's not strings attached to a degree /
After all, I am not your eternal pedigree /
You are covertly free /
To try out other people /
Perhaps get intimate with a couple /
Entangling your soul with strangers /
Ignoring the blaring dangers /
Of eroding your ability to stick /
While developing the mindset of a tick /
The search for a host to suck /
The life out of to nourish /
Your life inward /

It's a numbers game talk /
Yet I'd rather stumble upon the luck of this draw /
Knowing her flaws will be raw /
Knowing loving is still the law /

LXXXVII

The missing chunks of my heart /
Were stolen not by monsters /
But lovers and friends /

Would it be okay if /
I love you heartless?
Would it be enough if /
I give you the empty void in my chest?

Would it be okay if /
I look into your eyes, with the coldness of mine?
Would it be warm enough /
To keep you interested?

I promise you /
You will be safe /
You will have a whole rib cage /
To yourself, there would be no limits /

I promise you /
You would feel things you have never felt before /
You won't have to worry about expressing anything to me /
You would finally be happy /
Having it all without any responsibility towards me /

And when you have had your fill /
You would be able to move on to /
Someone you truly desire /
Without giving back in pieces /
What you never had in whole /

LXXXVIII

Mom: a nurturer /
All babies are born with one /
Her sacrifices begin at first cry /
Not yours, but hers /
Cries to be loved unconditionally at a day old /
It never stops till she dies /

Her sacrifices continue with /
Loving you unconditionally /
It never stops till she dies /

Her sacrifices end with making sure /
You are loved unconditionally /
By someone else /
It never stops, never will...

LXXXIX

Dear Miss /
He is a broken fixer /
That doesn't know what to fix /
So he is trying to fix you /
So his life can be fixed /

Dear Mister /
She is broken /
That's your token /
To take the lead you must /
By fixing yourself first /
Then decide...

It's like experiencing hygge /
Without good hygiene /
You want to come close /
Yet you don't want to get too close /
For the fear of being found out /
You keep intimacy locked out /

XC

Why would I ghost you?

I want forever, you want for now /
You want forever, I want for now /
I want forever, you don't want I /
You want forever, I don't want you /

You taking too much space without giving enough time /
You taking too much time, yet asking for space /
You are aloof, passively wishing I'd be active /
You want the pursuit that only suits you /

I want forever, you not giving value /
You want forever, I am not giving value /
I want forever, you not receiving value /
You want forever, I am not receiving value /

You taking too much space in my thoughts /
Without having space in my heart /
You are that relationship /
That just couldn't grow any further /

You are that pursuit that leads to a dead end /
You once said it will never happen /
Yet you keep tugging on my strings /
Waiting for your phone to ring /

I stopped talking /
And you stopped asking /
You stopped talking /
And I stopped asking /

I ghosted you because forever was never in the picture /
Desire will never be negotiated /

XCI

If we all measured our monies /
In terms of time /

Time required to make it /
Time required to gather it /
Time required to transport it /
Time required to grow it /
Time required to multiply it /
Time before it's finished /

We would realize we really don't have /
Much time to waste it /

I can tell you your soul is unhealthy /
By how you handle your money /

I have been there /
I know that feeling /

If you have insecurities /
You'll spend more /
On the lesser things /
That have the greatest hype /

XCII

Come over tonight /
Undress your heart /

Let me paint images /
Upon the canvas of your mind /

XCIII

I want to enjoy the fragrance /
Of your presence /
Without words /
The mingling of playful birds /
Singing new songs /
Embracing the love that belongs /
To the heart that longs for something strong /

XCIV

Love is /
Giving yourself wholly to your craft /
Facing your fears, embracing yourself /

The wordless feeling of being known /
Accepted, heard, understood, supported /

Giving us away wholly without expecting /
It to return wholly /

You /
Accepting you, respecting you /
Protecting you, embracing you /
Always /

XCV

Dear mind of mine /
I mind the fact that you mind /
However, I do mind /
When you don't want heart's desires /

All you have said is /
"What if this, what if that, /
What about this, what about that?"

I have a question for you /
What if you just shut up, sit back and relax /
Because heart and I are doing this /

XCVI

Everyone is a gift /
Yes! Everyone /
Respect them as you go along your journey /
It doesn't matter if you agree with them or not /
It doesn't matter if you like them or not /
It doesn't matter if you accept them or not /

Because /

You never know /
Or fully understand what they have been through /
You don't know what they are going through /

Owe no man anything than to love /

XCVII

This debate within is over /
I hate to say but I am pulling over /
To the side of unconditional love /
Like it was dealt to me from above /

It's my identity /
I'm a love entity /
God is my indemnity /
Against all odds till eternity /

Other opinions /
Got me layered up like an onion /
Causing others tears /
Just to hide my fears /
That shouldn't be what a man brings /
Never is it the attribute of true kings /

XCVIII

Sometimes /
There is nothing to write /
And it's not writer's block /

It's the calm /
Every writer needs to rediscover /
Who they really are /

It's the muse /
Screaming /

"You have lost yourself /
Find yourself outside your art" /

XCIX

Craving you /
Desires like an inferno /
Imploding, exploding /
Devouring me /

Let me /
Quench my voracious appetite /

Spread out your wings /
An invitation to /
Consume what's hidden between /

To eat into your heart /

Heartbeats in sync with vibrations /
Erupting inspirations /
Collapsing perspiration /

C

Look into my eyes – see /
The fire burning within my soul /
Tell me if I'm cold /
Feel me /
Forget what you've been told /

CI

Rain, rain, please don't go away /
Stay with me yet another day /
The fields of daises are ours to lay /

You said you would never go away /
Forever your love is here to stay /
Through changing seasons stormy and grey /
Together till we're old, I pray /

You are the light that makes my dark bright /
My delight that never goes out of sight /
If loving you is wrong, I don't wanna be right /
For perfect love never cherishes fright /

Rain, rain, soak me up in your showers /
Watering my seeds, I give you new flowers /
Uprooting the weeds that devour /
Nurturing the garden of eternal stay overs...

CII

"Sometimes you gotta shake things up real hard /
Before it goes too far, too soon /
Honesty brings reality into view faster than being nice" /

With a graceful gait /
He walked towards the gate /
Aware of the tightness of the air /
In her eyes, he couldn't see his heir /
He couldn't scream aloud /
For a man these days, that isn't allowed /
She wanted him to be wild, yet cuddly as a bear /
Contradicting traits he could hardly bear /

He knew he wasn't her one /
Yet she wanted him to be won /
She offered it piece by piece /
He whispered "this isn't peace" /
He needed to pray /
As he had fallen prey /
To the one who had nothing to sell /
To keep him locked in a cell /

Too late, being nice won't make bail /
With windows opened, he couldn't bail /
She knew he was a curious soul /
Who just realized he had been sold /
For a price that isn't fair /
Yet he would have to pay the fare /
To hold that which isn't dear /
This should never be a dare /

Tranquility he thought he would find /
Every step he took had him fined /
Her touch took him higher above the ceiling /
Little did he know, his heart was getting a sealing /
With the body of an eight /
Every week, his soul she ate /
He became weak, she became full /
While she considered him a fool /
For falling for the waist /
That wanted his life to waste /

By lust, she has him led /
More dangerous than poisoning with lead /
He had to make things right /
A new story he would have to write /
Of how he became a knight /
Through the darkest of night /

He had the pain lessen /
By learning this bitter lesson /
Being idle reveals an idol /
That to wait is a way to weigh /
All things that seem whole /
Yet drags you into a hole /

That to say no is to know /
Love for hire won't take you any higher /
That sometimes that which heals /
Requires you first take to your heels /

Because that untamed pleasure in your vein /
Leads you to all things vain /

Now his curious desires he fully knew /
All things suddenly became new /
For some things you learn by reading a book /
But understand by going through /

To those I have been honest with too soon /
I was only preventing fantasies from being sown /

Because I understand my weakness /
More than your meekness /

And to say I know you more than you /
Would be a self-deception redo /

CIII

You taught me to weather the storm /
Since the day I was born /
To Your heart, I belonged /
Even in wilderness years, lonely and long /

Fighting monsters, beasts and ghosts /
Liberating soul from foreign hosts /
Always remembering Your Word is a lamp to my feet /
Hands clenched to my swords, my eyes won't see defeat /

There are things you get born into /
Others over time are birthed into... you /
My battles had turned me into a shapeshifter /
Always adapting, never a mindless drifter /

CIV

Some friends remind me /
Never to settle for mediocre relationships /

The ones that check on you /
The ones that make you smile /
The ones that initiate a part of your day /
The ones that choose you over and over again /

For the best gift you can give a person /
Is the gift of quality time /

CV

I do care /
Enough to know /
Sometimes /
I don't care /
Enough to know /
I do care /

However /
I don't care /
Because /
Most times /
I would care /
Enough to know /
I do care /
Too much /
I won't care /
At all /
And still /
You wouldn't care /
Enough to know /
You don't care /
At all /

And /
The truth is /
I don't care at all /

CVI

It's Your name /
That freed me from shame /
It's Your fame /
That ignited my flame /
It's Your reign /
That blesses me with rain /

Nourishing my seeds /
Purifying my deeds /
Providing my needs /
Truth my soul feeds /

In You, my heart is prancing /
With You, I am dancing /

CVII

Silence is poetic too /

CVIII

When I walk through the valley of... /

"What the f... is this?" /

That realm that is beyond /
Logic and reasoning...
When I cannot make sense of it all /
The only logic and reasoning I know is /

"You are good and you love me" /

CIX

Your blood splattered /
On the walls of my heart /
Filling up those deep crevices /
Created by words that battered /
My childlike innocence /

The pressures of life leave me unbalanced /
Yet, You see more of me through Your lens /
Sometimes I wonder if it's the lustre /
In Your eyes You see in mine /

"I am yours", You whisper... /

CX

Loving Hands /
Carefully stitching /
Torn pieces together /

To Himself /
Eternally inseparable /

So, all the more I rejoice /
For I have found joy /
In my brokenness /

CXI

Sex for pleasure /
Pleasure like leisure /
Leisure without further intentions /
Intentions devoid of lasting tomorrow /
Tomorrow when there is a change in taste /
Tastes begging for companionship and intimacy /
Intimacy transforming into neediness /
Neediness crying out for grace /
Grace to taste something sacred /
Sacred beyond sex /

CXII

I hear you say:

"Cry on my shoulders /
Tears, snorts and all /
Always near /
Even when you don't call /
Helping you carry the weight that bothers /
With simple words said in a prayer" /

Listen to me:

"Your heart shouldn't be in a snare /
Made by those who sneer /
My love for you will always bear /
The moments your soul experiences tears /

I am your friend:

Always waiting to hear /
How you are feeling, dear /
For you are closer than a friend /
Your heart we will defend /
Never leaving you at any bend /
Let's contend for this season to end /

CXIII

Hurry and be sorry /
Waiting is weighty /
It doesn't matter who?!
You'll be sorry, boo /
I never judge a book /
By how it should look /
I wait in front of it /
Observing what may hint /
Then I open the first and last page /
Everything in between changes with age /
You were a restless book /
With a very calm look /
If I had opened you gently /
Your pages would have flown away endlessly /
Those who don't learn to wait /
End up becoming bait /

CXIV

I cannot fix you /
You cannot fix me /

I want the best for you /
You want the best for me /

What if the best we seek /
Is love bearing up under all things /

Would you take my hands?
Would your heart be free falling?
Would you stop being pressed for time?

CXV

For I am no longer ashamed /
Of what's broken on the inside /
For I see Your loving Hands /
Leaving Your divine Fingerprints /
Even on those disconnected pieces /

Even those shards /
Reflect the beauty of who You are /
In me /

I am aware /
I am no longer ashamed /

CXVI

When brittle hearts /
Whisper to soft hearts /
"Get over it" /
Why is your heart so broken?
Pain is life's token /

I laugh at their trust /
In a tap that is so rust /
Every turn squeaks /
Every hose leaks /
When pressure peaks /

I'm not fooled by your strength /
You can't withstand the length /
For hearts that are truly strong /
Are never entirely wrong /
About how long it will take /
For a broken heart to make /
Its way back to wholeness /
Where it embraces boldness /

Hearts that really heal are tough /
Your hardness of heart isn't enough /

CXVII

Crashed eagle /
Beak's broken /
Ribs crushed /
Wings torn /

Lying still upon this mountain /
Watching the sun rise and set /
Hoping to soar once again /
Upon the winds of the morning /

Battle eagle /
The talons are growing /
Into serrated blades /
As the memories of old fades /

Oh, my soul /
You will soar again /
Healing is happening /
Let patience wrap you with kindness /

CXVIII

Your heart is far more precious than rubies /
Not to be found in the hands of wannabes /
Remember love is first patient and kind /
Give yourself space to grow your mind /

A boy who hasn't found himself isn't worthy of your dignity /
For he is a shattered soul drowning in the waters of ambiguity /

He will leave you shattered in tiny pieces /
Pronouncing you guilty /
He will blame you /
Holding you accountable for his heart's disunity /

Your heart is far more precious than rubies /
Don't you know you are God's own beauty?
Let no one keep you gloomy /
Loving you is God's cherished duty /

CXIX

*To those who say you can't, f*** them!*
You will make them scream damn!
Because you are pure fire /
Let no one put out your heart's desire /

People always reject what they don't understand /
Saying you can't do this, that and...
However, they don't need to see what you see in yourself /
Deeper into self-discovery allow your heart to delve /

For you are a vessel of great power /
Let no one's view bring you lower /
God is knitting you piece by piece /
Let your heart be at peace /

CXX

Benefits /
Like chords /
With thorns sharp /
Perforating their fragile souls /
Continuously /

Benefits /
Like chords /
Entangling, pleasurable, suffocating /
Jealously brews a poisonous /
Drink /

Benefits /
Bittersweet /
Adventure without destination /
A highway going ultimately /
Nowhere /

CXXI

You pursue me /
Like You need me /
When I am the one /
Who is in need of You /

For love is the ability to see value in another /
And the willpower to protect /celebrate such value /

Our love is like a ring /
No beginning, no end /
Forever is all it brings /
Nothing else contends /

CXXII

Nice people are just afraid of being good /
So, they coexist with the things they don't agree with /
They compromise their values /
Or belief systems for the sake of peace /

They become agreeable, politically correct /
Easily influenced by environments that have nothing to do with where they want
to be /
Sadly walking around with broken narratives /

Instead of respectfully disagreeing /
They disrespect their own heart by agreeing /
Thus, becoming really confused about life itself /

Being good is chaotic in nature, unfortunately /

CXXIII

Host me, Holy Ghost host /
Host me, Holy Ghost host /

You, my friend, are not like most /
You, my friend, are not like most /

My heart will forever raise a toast /
Louder than the strongest boast /
For Jesus who died on a post /
For transgressions justifiable for a roast /

Host me, Holy Ghost host /
You, my friend, are not like most /

CXXIV

Dear Hopeless Romantic /

Hope less in romanticism as an expression of true love /
Hope more in practicality mixed with virtue /
A by-product of faithfulness /

Don't get it twisted /
That good boy is still human /
That good girl is still human /
When it comes to it /
They will fight for themselves first /

Yours faithfully /
Practical decisions /

CXXV

Lord /
Keep my heart hungry for You /
For there is a familiarity that leads to pride /
Guard my heart /
Let me not lose the childlike wonder of You /
For to be matured in You is to be like a child /
Crying out "Abba" /
Knowing You are my fortress, my sustenance /
Even my father David, a valiant warrior /
Still wept before You, seeking Your face /
In times of need /

CXXVI

You are there /
You are always there /
To protect, nurture, feed /
Some say You are sensitive /
Yes, sensitive to the fluctuations /
Of our hearts, for You love deeply /
Never wanting us to wander off /
You give us a lot /
Whether we ask or not /
Whether we accept or not /
In Your free gift we find strength /
To go through the ridiculous /
Moments of life /
Coming out fabulous /
Without who You are /
There is no fulfilment in life /
For You are the eternal peace /
That connects the pieces of /
All of our endeavours together /
Even when we are plagued by /
Guilt, shame, regrets /
You are still loving /
Immerse us in patience /
Encouraging us to have lots of patience /
With ourselves /
And when we choose to ignore /
The things that are toxic to us /
You are the gentle, honest whisper /
That convicts us with grace /
If God is the father of us all /
I know Holy Spirit, You are Mommy /
For that is what moms do /

CXXVII

Love can neither be created nor destroyed /
It only gets passed on from one person to the next /

However, there is a type of love /
No human can create /
Except it is given by the divine /
Even that, only a few discover /

That is what I search for /
Agape!

For Agape sees every day as new /
Requiring new faith, new hope, new mercies /

CXXVIII

Oh! That timeless masterpiece /
Whose words and stories /
Mentor me in this game called life /

For I asked it a question /
"What do you do after love has said no?"
Men tell me to pursue still /
To show her she's worth more /

But the Bible says:

"Ghost her, get into community, improve yourself" /

CXXIX

Self-righteousness like an armour /
Protects the rot on the inside from oozing /
On the outside /
Perhaps if we exposed our imperfections /
Maybe the rot would finally burn under the light /

Well /
Without empathy /
It will only produce more self-righteousness and indulgence /

So I /

Light a fire within /burning it all up /

CXXX

After all /
At the end /
Love never fails /
For the man / woman who truly fails /
Is the one who hasn't learned /
How to love /

Unfortunately /

Love isn't a feeling /
But a decision /
To deal with the false layers /
Till our eyes can /
Finally see /

CXXXI

If /
Love was fire /
I want to burn in it /
Till it aspires desires /

To love /
The unlovable /
On the inside /
Of me /
Till it inspires desire /
To love /
The unlovable /
Outside /
Of me /

God /
Give me the grace to do it /
Regardless of how I feel it /
In order to be it /

CXXXII

In love, I'm born /
I'm worn /
I'm torn /
No, I won't turn /
Away from the churn /
I'd rather be in an urn /
Than be without love's burn /

CXXXIII

The struggles between /
Doing the right things /
And doing things right /
Tears one apart /
So much /
I no longer want to be right /

Yet a right without /
Faith, Hope and Love /
Is wrong /

Something without love /
Does not belong /

CXXXIV

And then /
There are those who erupt on the inside /
Calling those who erupt on the outside /
Emotional /
It's that corrupt state of mind /
Where our self-righteousness /
Shames others /
For their self-indulgence /
Forgetting we are all self-aware /

Of the shit that goes on within /

Well, I am aware of my own /
Don't know how you ignore your drown /
Thinking you have grown /

In it all /
We are all beautiful art /

CXXXV

What is love, I ask /
The presence /
To which my soul finally basks /

You are the fire /
Forever all-consuming /
Soothing to my soul /

Without You, no me /
You are my totality /
We are one, always /

CXXXVI

You are beauty personified /
The warmth from your gaze leaves me fried /
Sometimes I wonder if you can cool it down a little /
Yet it's what makes you wild, not gentle /
I love that you are authentic /
It's what makes your heart thick /
Your natural abilities to be tough yet soft /
Contradicting traits that can't be bought /
Yet again I find myself lost in thoughts /
Coming in successions so oft /
Of why you feel you are not all that /
Someone please whack her with a bat /
Perhaps it's another case of loose screws /
Or these words need time to brew /

CXXXVII

No woman had a firm grip on him /
For no matter how in love he was /
He had a way with himself /
That seems to make /
Even the tightest grip slip off /

For he had learned to bleed oil /
In the midst of the pressure /

CXXXVIII

So, they concluded we were weird /
I think they were beyond wired /
I don't claim to be normal /
I just think their perspectives are abnormal /
For how can you tell me to be mediocre /
Is the road to excellence without being a joker /
Now you are wondering what I mean /
Love should never create a heated scene /
To each other we should all be nice /
Freezing the darkness within in ice /
That our private lives should be made public /
Turning our families into a republic /
Where we no longer have a say in how we should grow /
Because somehow y'all are always in the know /
I try to stay away from the status quo /
Don't need to create a reality from a senseless quote /

CXXXIX

That change occurs when you are alone /
Because without others you will find your home /
How else do we discover when we belong /
If we don't embrace what has been there all along /
How do you then, strengthen the rational /
If you don't confront the darkness that is emotional /
What is truth then?
If it cannot give hope to the loneliness in your den /
I think collectively we want failure /
So, we encourage each other towards the comfort that lures /
Hoping individually, one will find success /
So, it can be shared with others in excess /
So, we chant together that we are brave /
Alone, the coward only craves /
Without coming to terms with this fact /
That makes up our social art /
Together we shield each other from the pain /
The only path that leads to gain /
We create bonds of pleasure /
Finding depths in all things leisure /
Yet we know it isn't the measure of life /
Neither is it the depths we truly want to dive /
For such connection is only temporary /
When the night falls, we are hungry on the contrary /
Because you can't feed what is eternal /
By ignoring the desires internal /
So, we make war thinking it's fair /
And cry out for peace when it's unfair /
We embrace regress calling it progress /
By creating a cult without developing our internal culture /
We start a war between the masculine and the feminine /
Thinking it will produce a cure /

CXL

Cry on my shoulders /
Tears, snorts and all /
Always near, even when you don't call /
Helping you carry the weight that bothers /
With simple words said in a prayer /
Your heart never meant to be in a snare /
My love for you will always bare /
The moments your soul is in a tear /
Always waiting to hear /
How you are feeling, dear /
For you are closer than a friend /
Your heart we will defend /
Never leaving you at any bend /
Let's contend /
For this season to end /

CXLI

I remember when I muted those pages /
Trying to protect my abstinence in stages /
I was the boy who played with matches /
Without knowing that desire latches /

Now I know better /
Naked images are bitter /
Those things that glitter /
Don't make you get her /

Keep fanning their flames /
While drowning them in blames /
In the end, you will get your scars /
While they remain part of your past /

My greatest regret was an insecurity /
That developed a wrong curiosity /
Leading me on the path of vain precocity /
Shackled by my mind's atrocity /

CXLII

You are a gift /
Your love gives a lift /
To those caught in a drift /
Rescuing them with your wit /
In my heart, you fit /
To me, you are sweet /

CXLIII

You feel like a mess /
Yet, you are a beautiful princess /
Winning the process of success /
'Cos winning is your business /
Even in the face of distress /
You confront it like a tigress /
With the wisdom to address /
Even in the midst of stress /

CXLIV

Try to survive /
Love will revive /
You will thrive /
Soaring into height /

Your broken wings will heal /
No matter how you feel /
Don't take to your heel /
Face the giant with might /

Your roar will be the last sound heard /
All of your insecurities will all be dead /
You will take flight like a mighty war bird /
Each feather in your wings will produce light /

I know it's been a long hard road /
With stories that cannot be told /
Tonight it's okay to fold /
Knowing yesterday isn't your last fight /

For this reason /
You will not stay here /
Your fight will not end in tears /
You will grow into greatness /

CXLV

I have found what I was missing /
My love was growing smaller /
For to love less is an impossible solution /
Leading to intense apathy /
What a joyful sadness /
To cease being a living sacrifice /
Yet it was my only choice /
To keep myself from crash landing /
A truth deceptively honest /
Leading to an extinct life /
The embrace of a comfortable misery /
Thumping with thundering whispers /
Of look at you; you screwed up /
Was it gonna be okay to be openly deceptive?
Staging a peaceful conquest /
While my mind shrieks from silent screams /
Creating a static flow /

CXLVI

Dear writer's block /

You got my attention /
By selling me perfection /
Eating deep like an infection /

I will ignore your rules /
Don't wanna hear your blues /
I write, that's cool /

I am on the fifth one /
And it's barely 30 mins /
Makes me question /
If you are even a thing /

Are you really a thing /
Or something made up /
To express when writers /
Let their minds choke up /
Their own hearts /

CXLVII

Look /
Through the /
Eyes of faith /
What do you see /
Now /

Now /
Take that /
Feel it till /
It overwhelms you deeply /
Today /

Today /
I don't /
Want you saying /
Anything that is contrary /
Again /

Love /
Is always /
Kind you find /
To love without caring /
Impossible /

Impossible /
Things are /
Possible through faith /
See beyond your mindsets /
Seriously /

Seriously /
Think about /
What you think /
Is the way to /
Love /

Love /
Isn't need /
You want something /
For reasons known to /
You /

You /
Only want /
To fulfill needs /
After fulfillment, what next /
Love /

Love /
Is not /
Just a feeling /
But a person with /
Identity /

Identity /
Is everything /
Who you think /
You are is important /
Always /

Always /
Remember you /
Won't find love /
Anywhere you don't see /
Love /

Love /
Won't see /
You if you /
Don't see you as /
Love /

Love /
Everyone is /
Looking for love /
Why haven't they found /
You /

You /
Would think /
It's because we /
Are all somewhat blind /
Right /

Right /
Blind to /
The love on /
The inside of us /
Always /

Always /
Faith is /
Identity built within /
Words becoming a reality /
Continuously /

Continuously /
Speak over /
Yourself the things /
You desire in another /
Else /

Else /
You keep /
Feeling incomplete with /
Others thinking you are /
Lacking /

Speaking /
Of lack /
What do you /
Think you are lacking /
Now /

Now /
Imagine you /
Have only two /
Options to choose from /
Okay /

Okay /
To create /
Or okay to /
Wait for it to /
Come /

Come /
Into the /
Confidence that which /
Ever you choose is /
Right /

Right /
For where /
You are at /
No matter what you /
Feel /

Feel /
Contented with /
Yourself for choosing /
To create or wait /
Today /

Today /
You get /
To decide stillness /
Over the desire to /
Have /

Have /
What you /
Don't have now /
Stillness of heart regardless /
If /

If /
The desire /
Is met or /
Not met now or /
Today /

Today /
Who told you /
You were incomplete /
You told yourself those /
Lies /

Lies /
Are truths /
Lacking a future /
Should you be its /
Future?!

Future /
You is /
Truth filled you /
Today, not yesterday or /
Tomorrow /

Tomorrow /
Has not /
Been formed yet /
It isn't waiting for /
You /

You /
Need to /
Decide if you /
Will catch up to /
It /

It /
Will only /
Honour what you /
Decide to do with /
Today /

Today /
You will /
Do these things /
Make a clean cut /
Immediately /

Immediately /
Forget the /
Past, faith isn't /
There, forget the future /
Too /

Too /
Often we /
Think faith is /
For the future we /
See /

See /
Faith is /
The evidence of /
Things unseen at present /
Now /

Now /
Can you /
Find faith in /
A moment not yet /
Alive /

Alive /
You must /
Be this moment /
For faith is present /
Now /

How /
You ask?
How do I /
Make that cut with /
Reality /

Reality /
Is made /
Of the words /
You speak to you /
Others /

Others /
Speak words /
To you also /
Words are not truth /
What?!

What /
Are words /
Then?! Words are /
Words, a means of /
Communication /

Communication /
Is access /
From one entity /
To another to experience /
Dimensions /

Dimensions /
Not visible /
But actively creating /
The visible through the /
Invincible /

Invincible /
Doesn't mean /
Non existing but you /
Cannot see it yet /
Okay /

Okay /
Now you /
Understanding the importance /
Of speaking the right /
Words /

Words /
Are things /
Think about everything /
Around you that contains /
Those /

CXLVIII

Few knew we threw the new /
That is skew to view the new /
That is true, for we grew the new /
That is due and slew the new /
That screw the glue of the new /
That flew away, shoo that new hue /
In lieu of you that has a clue /
Why the wind blew a direction new /
And go with that which drew /
Your heart towards the new crew /
And not the news that brews and stews /
That which isn't new /

CXLIX

As I confront my childhood pains /
Taking off all the masks /
My heart asks /
Why did we do this anyway?
I replied /
We were trying to hide in every way /
For my childhood mind couldn't comprehend why /
So, we used a greater pain /
To numb a lesser pain /

Now the greater pain is the monster /
Stuck in the mirror on the inside /
This time no shortcuts /
Sorry but no girl courts /
Until the dark knight within rises /
I will not pay shallow prices /
Of conformity and compromise /

CL

Reaching for the crown /
Fighting what's weighing me down /
I won't give up /
Accepting this is my cup /
Who said I'm drowning /
Who said I'm frowning /
Those who will be at my enthroning /
For it's the season of my glowing /
You can't hear my groaning /
Muffled up whispers of painful moaning /
As these dark waters cover still /
I will reach out until I breathe through my sweat pores /
Taking in the air life stores /
Till the stars see my hands /
Reaching out above this flowing land /
I won't drown here in this uncertainty /
For You are my crown forever into eternity /

CLI

Loving her is like /
Recreating warmth /

She reminds me of /
Coffee /
A strong presence permeating /
My atmosphere /

Let us squeeze out /
What is left of this love /
Before we step into the abyss /
Of craving what we never had /

CLII

She built walls /
Thick enough to keep him out /

She snuck through the back door /
In search for kin that won't let her in /

She offered them free gifts /
While waiting for him to pay a price /

She had gotten accustomed /
To the sweet melodies of his knocks /

She was oblivious /
To the moment when the music stopped /

CLIII

In my past /
I saw you last /
To you, I was an outcast /
To me, you were the cast /
Wearing different faces /
Giving different embraces /
Of a friend and a traitor /
You were my love tutor /
I was your suitor /
You were the stator /
I was the rotor /
Always revolving around you /
Never resolving to be away from you /

Until now /

CLIV

Your love is like giant sparks of energy /
Invading my atmosphere /
My heart letting out thunderous claps /
Shaking the biosphere /
Losing control so fast /
Without care /
Your admiration was devoid /
Of fear /

Now on that day /
Her right atmosphere was lured /
With each other we felt...
I thought we were finally secured /
Didn't know I was used as a solution to an itch /
Begging to be cured /
Your presence filled with incomplete half-truths /
That lead hearts obscured /

Yet I am drowned in this longing to return to you /
Whet feels like a myth /
When love and indifference collide /
What's left is worse than filth /
I find myself embracing /
The possibilities of odious /
Knowing the truth we hide /
Is superficial /

CLV

If confidence was the incident /
My dear, this love is an accident /

For I have been in my skin /
Faithfully doing this love thing /
Regardless of what you think /

I remember the first time /
I got caught in your gaze /
Watching a billion gases /
Burning in sacred union /
Your hugs felt like succulent /
Layers from spicy onions /
My heart wouldn't relent /
Regardless of teary opinions /

Yet this isn't what you want /
It's simple with nothing to flaunt /
Not as dangerous as a wild hunt /

If confidence was the incident /
My dear, what we have is an accident /

CLVI

Like a bird, he had caged her /
Like a slave, he had managed her /
Like a broken song, he had damaged her /

My skin is soaked with her tears /
When I close my eyes I see her fears /
Her heart always screams, no one cares /

What the fuck is wrong with men these days /
The jerk race no longer marathons but relays /
Consuming without awareness of how her heart lays /

She is my friend, my buddy /
I told her to run away, and I ain't sorry /
I ain't telling you where she is /
You don't have to worry /

Everyone deserves a new start /
Distance and space to create a new heart /
Discovering new ways to learn how to fight /

Take flight, my dear, take flight /
Run fast, run far, don't return /

Create that home in the distant /
You've always told me about /

I'll be your warrior friend /
Guarding your secret to the end /

Let your broken wings heal /
Watching every tissue seal /

Soar, my dear, into greater heights /
Love yourself, shine your hidden lights /

You are beautiful, my friend /
You'll always be to the end /

Do not return to his brokenness /
Let him fight his own darkness /

CLVII

You are always the villain /
Irrespective of where you choose to be in your lane /
For the good guys /
Are beasts in the eyes of the bad guys /

Every battle ends in cries /
Memories of loss till the blood dries /
Even darkness has a lot to say /
When tortured by what light has got to say /

The devil has me in a double cross /
Yet Jesus won me with a cross /
He taught me to pray /
So I don't end up becoming prey /

CLVIII

Close /
Come close /
Close enough /
To hear your heart /
SING /

Gaze /
You gaze /
Gaze into /
Me forever /
LOVE /

Sink /
Let sink /
Sink into /
Wholesome loving /
NOW /

CLIX

The face that froze your phase /
Without regard for your pace /
Withholding grace /
Entangling you in lace /
Ending your race /
Like it was a waste to figure out your maze /
You got dizzy /
So easy you got lazy and fizzy /
lost in a universe diverse /
And perverse you searched for a verse to hit reverse /
In order to converse or converge, yet you are on the verge /
Of falling off the ledge, hitting the edge /
A merge with the earth /
Ending in death /

CLX

Not your style /
Not your hype /
Not your type /

I need you to know /
Your heart matters /
So does mine /

Walk away, walk on /

Your style /
Hype /
Type /
Is within you /

So /

Walk away, walk on /

CLXI

Summer things /
Warmer flings /
Skimpy clothes /
Skipping hearts /

Show me some skin /
Leaking sweat /
Like sipping gin /

Forgetting the frost bite /
Of last winter's sting /

CLXII

There is a pull within me /
Towards that which is divine /
An unexplainable hunger for God /
And all things supernatural /
Pulling me away from the crowd /
Letting me drown in silence /
Until I am completely submerged /
In that secret place /
Where it's all supernatural gain /
Supernaturally Him /

CLXIII

The real guy woke up one morning /
Frustrated, broken, fed-up /
He went to the backyard /
And dug up that buried shotgun "anger" /
His first target was the nice guy /
Shot him in the head /
Pushed him down the stairs /
His next was his environment /
He couldn't murder them all /
For they did nothing wrong /
So he jumped over the fence of opinions /
And ventured into the unknown /
Changing his perspectives /
And narratives one step at a time /
He gets to a pool of water /
Seeing his reflection /
He smiled for he saw the guy /
Whose identity wasn't defined by anyone /
The good guy /

CLXIV

This means war /
You can hear me roar /
My love ready to pour /
Your heart ready to soar /

Your mind will rattle /
As you sink into this battle /
Taking in mind mindful pounds /
Giving off deep whispered sounds /

Say anything you want /
Why are you looking so burnt? /
After all, you had a body to flaunt /
Common beauty inspiring a vaunt /

Round two has begun /
After this, I'll be gone /
You never wanted to be the one /
My heart was never won /

To your friends you tattled /
Saying I wasn't your type, I'm startled /
I pursued you to bring you in as my wife /
But you went and brought you a knife /

Now this means war /
You cannot hear me roar /
My wrath ready to pour /
Too bad, you don't know what's in store /

CLXV

I want you to lead /
Yet she won't lead herself to /
Follow him

It's like dragging /
A heavy drum of water /
Uphill to pour it downhill /

CLXVI

For better or worse /
When love songs turn blue /
I am always yours /

Once sweet voices, now coarse /
Nothing left to throw, but a shoe /
I am always yours /

Good reasons to set a new course /
Remind me before picking a new boo /
For better or worse /

Love can feel like a curse /
With a lot of bitterness to spew /
I am always yours /

It's okay to take a pause /
Let's search for a new view /
For better or worse /

Rip me to shreds with claws /
We are stuck together like glue /
I am always yours /

This is my own clause /
This is my only due /
For better or worse /
I am always yours /

CLXVII

I'll do anything /
For some time /
With you /

You're my everything /
With or without a rhyme /
I'll do anything /

I'll do all things /
For a love full-time /
With you /

It's a beautiful thing /
For a lifetime /
I'll do anything /

The memories ring /
The taste of sweet wine /
With you /

It's the love that springs /
Growing in its prime /
I'll do anything /

In all things /
For all times /
I'll do anything /
With you /

CLXVIII

Let me finger your mind with a pole /
A magical curvy pen with great girth /
Engraving my poetry into your soul /

Let me scribble songs upon your scroll /
Tongues engaging in sneaky frolic mirth /
Let me finger your mind with a pole /

Let's create desire burning like coal /
With the simple things upon this earth /
Engraving my poetry into your soul /

Making you gush is the ultimate goal /
Screams, tears like the day of your birth /
Let me finger your mind with a pole /

Let's redeem the attention you stole /
The day you unveiled your mind's worth /
Engrave your poetry into my soul /

Swallow all of my verses whole /
From Calgary down to Perth /
Let me finger your mind with a pole /
Engraving my poetry into your soul /

CLXIX

Constant one; whom I love deeply /
Your beauty in creation; so loud, they cannot be ignored /
You stand so close, You can't be ignored /
You remain still; gently tapping me on the shoulders /
By the generous display of Your grace /
Abundant in my weakness /
Your overflowing joy in me becomes my strength /
Ah! I proclaim louder everyday /
I can do all things through Your Son who strengthens me /
With You I can scale a fence /
In You I do unimaginable things /

When my soul seems darker /
Than the icy winter nights /
Getting caught in the entanglements of wrongful doings /
Ravaged by dangerous desires like a city without walls /
Desiring stolen water, drinking from polluted cisterns /
You stand so close, You can't be ignored /
You remain still; gently tapping me on the shoulders /
By the warmth of Your burning love /
Suffering long with me, You never give up on my process /
Always reminding me of the crown of victory You have reserved / For me /
Your gentleness in me becomes my inspiration /
To surrender constantly /
Walking towards Your mercy /

When my heart breaks /
By the drifting possibilities of a reality that felt so real /
Of promises written in stone that seem to weather away /
Of a cloud of hope, that was and now isn't /
Of a faith, with roots too weak to go any deeper /
Of a gift that walks out the door /
You stand so close, You can't be ignored /
You remain still; gently tapping me on the shoulders /
By the comfort of Your spirit on the inside of me /
Reminding me it's okay to cry, it's okay to feel the pain /
For You are my gain /
And each season is not in vain /
For You work all things together to give me /
A renewed hope that creates a future rich in Your divine nature /

When my pocket seems dry /
And I am reminded of all the things I desire to have /
But cannot have; my needs that I cannot meet /
You stand so close, You can't be ignored /
You remain still; gently tapping me on the shoulders /
Reminding me that You are more than enough for me /
My heart is content in now, with hope for tomorrow /
For You know all I need; You are my source /
All that I am, all that I will ever be is You /
You supply all my needs according to Your richness /
My net worth is Jesus /

When the house feels empty /
And I yearn for another to share the love You have given me with /
I wait impatiently for the beauty You have prepared for me /
I for her /
Knowing not what to do, or where to search /
When all the voices around tell me to go here and there /
And deep down, You remind me to stay still in You /
You remain still; gently tapping me on the shoulders /
For I know You are so close; I can't ignore You /
I remember I love You /
You are the anchor that keeps my heart still /
Even in the raging torrents of unexpressed emotions /
You are the light, that shines still /
At the end of the darkest tunnels of unending uncertainty /
You are the everlasting payment still /
Of an unplayable debt that I owed /
You are the administrator of my soul /
The keeper of my spirit /
The one who has made my body His eternal home /
You cannot be ignored /

CLXX

The fire of Your love /
Keeps me blazing /
Your grace, so amazing /
My eyes keep gazing /
At Your face, with every pace I make /
Each morning I wake /
I quake in knowing I'm accepted /
By the One who made it all and gave it all /
To have me all, makes me wanna hit the streets /
Raving, waving about Your goodness and kindness /
Even in my mess, You keep blessing me /

That You would relentlessly pursue me /
Even though I am the one with the issues /
My weaknesses don't faze You /
My junk and funk don't leave You punk'd /
Still You remain constant in every instance /
No gaps in all laps, I clap for You my champion /
My Lion, my friend till the end /

Eternal love /
What else can be compared /
On and on it goes, on and on /
No separation, no divide /
You see beauty even in my imperfections /
Wholeness in my brokenness /
I am amazed, I'm so amazed /
That You would choose me as Your lover /
Patiently looking into my eyes /
Even when I get attracted by distractions /
That make me lose traction /
Your intentional gaze restores me into the chambers of /
Your kindness /
Caressing every inch of my skin with Your gentleness /
Till I'm sucked in once again, meshed into one piece with You /

Oh, that which divides lovers /
I pray that I may not be found by You /
That I may remain bonded to my perfect lover /
The One whose sweet kisses awakens my soul /
My soul exploding with joyful chants of praise /
To my King, my Saviour /
Majestic in all beauty, beauty raving in splendour /
Eyes blazing like fire, hair white as wool /
Your robe fills the temple /
What else, I say what else can be compared to You /
Everlasting pleasure...
In You, true delight is found /
Mercy and justice abound /
Oh perfect lover, once again /
I am swept away into that place /
Where words aren't enough to fully express...

CLXXI

Hearts tethered to You /
Always filled with hope anew /
If only we knew /
Our masks won't be painted blue /

Your voice calls us near /
"Let go of what you hold dear" /
Yet our minds are gripped by uncertain fears /
Drowning our pupils in a sea of tears /

Entangled in the realities of my longings /
Unquenchable thirsts swallowing up my belongings /
The search for my truest calling /
Has left me torn into pieces with endless bawling /

Perhaps I hide it all away in smiles /
Ignoring the blisters from walking for miles /
Looking for love devoid of truthful lies /
Instead of one tied like a kite that flies /

But /

My heart longs for You, my soul craves thee /
If it were left with me, I won't let the heavens be /
Until I am completely submerged in the arms of love /
Until You and I fit together like a glove /

CLXXII

Lord, You said you would /
Lord, You said You /
Lord, You said /
Lord, You!
Lord...

Still /
I /
I said /
I said, I /
I said, I will /
I said, I will follow /
I said, I will follow you /

For who else do I have apart from You /
Who has been with me since the beginning /
Alone in the abyss of darkness /
Who stood with me when my heart /
Was torn away from my chest /
Dropped on the concrete pavement /
Pierced with stilettos /
And left to bleed out /

You /
You, Lord /
You, Lord, made /
You, Lord, made me /
You, Lord, made me whole /

You are (insert your name)' s constant healer /
You are (insert your name)'s constant /
You are (insert your name)'s /
You are /
You /

CLXXIII

Hopelessness covers me like a cloak /
A ridicule to all I have become /
It was my fault, Lord /
I spoke of things I had no knowledge of /
Thinking it was Your rivers of wisdom flowing through me /

You have taught me in Your mercy /
You have shown me the foolishness of my own heart /
You have revealed to me the fundamentals of wisdom /
To be silent, to be quiet, to let revelation take root in my heart /
To let it find its expressions through my life /

I wanted to teach Your words Lord /
Without spending time at Your feet /
For it's easier to spew out words /
Than stew in the fire of devotion /

Yet again, I rejoice in Your mercy /
For the one whom the Lord does not correct /
Is the one truly perishing /
Whatever You say, Lord, I will do /
Wherever You ask, I will go /

I want You, I want all of You, Lord /
Let me not perish in the desires /
That does not profit a man's soul /
For You are the One my heart yearns for /

CLXXIV

God /
You are so constant /
Your words are true in every instant /
In every season /
You are the reason /
That keeps us going through the distance /

You are the face /
My heart will always embrace /
In every pace /
With you I never find disgrace /
In every race /
You embellish me with Your grace /

Therefore /

As the battles rage on /
We keep moving on /
Knowing we're Your warriors /
With You, nothing will worry us /
Cos Your love never ends /

Even though the valley is filled with thorns /
And our hearts bleed, Your spirit still intercedes /
We know in the end, we succeed, so we proceed /

CLXXV

You are the light /
That gives me a glow /
When I am low /
For in me You delight /
Even when I can't take flight /
You cover me in might /
Giving me the sight /
I need to see through twilight /

CLXXVI

The obstacle is the way /
The journey back into the path of greater resistance /
The attraction to what's easy, yet false in times of stress /
And hunger /
Is every warrior's greatest weakness /
The yearn for peace is what makes us settle /
For that which does not satisfy /
If love for God doesn't make a man fight his greatest battles /
I don't know what else will /

I will seek nothing less /
I will go through this darkness /
I will leap over those walls /
However many they are /
For nothing will separate God from my love /

CLXXVII

Life is a process /
It never got into recess /
God never sees you as useless /
Shaping you is His business /

God gives you life /
Filled with endless opportunities /
You only need to see endless possibilities /
In your own abilities /
To create with His words what He has given /
The life you want to be living /
By moving and believing /

CLXXVIII

You don't have to worry /
You don't have to be sorry /
You are only part of his story /
You won't lose sight of his glory /

Cause at the end of it all /
Your heart will not be left in a stall /
It's okay if today you cannot stand tall /
Remember you always recover from every fall /

CLXXIX

Conquered loneliness /
By falling in love with being alone /
For I suffered the fear of being lonely /
By being with others /

I had to push them all away /
To discover what I could give to me /
That no one else can give enough of /
Unconditional love and acceptance /

Now I love being alone /
Cos I am content with and full of divine love /
Without the need to belong somewhere or with someone /

For I was addicted to people /
I had a need to be needed /
Now I don't /
For there is more in ourselves to explore /
Than in others to devour /

CLXXX

I love you for you not for what you do /
Yet, for who you are /

Yet what you do is as important as who you are /
If we were to love others for a reason /
We won't love in all seasons /
For somedays are devoid of reasons /
Shall we then detach from what is out of season /

CLXXXI

I tried being a leader /
Discovered I was the worst follower /
For I am not a people-pleaser /
But much of a mind teaser /
For reality to me is only a fantasy appearing real /
If it's malleable by a mere change of what is ideal /

A simple story from various perspectives /
Can turn a man into a hero or villain without detectives /
Proving if the listeners are innocent or guilty /
How can we, when holding on to our narratives is a duty /
We get oppressed by their ideas /
They get liberated from what is ours /
Isn't that the game we play /
Thinking in everything us, they have say /
Thus, they want us to decay so they can grow /
Claiming they had to die so we would be in the know /

CLXXXII

The people calling us weird /
Are so strange /
They hide their hungers /
Claiming they're stronger /
We expose our hungers /
Uncovering the danger /
We are alone without feeling lonely /
Yet they call us lonely /
Because they can't be alone /

CLXXXIII

Why does it feel like flattery /
Why does it have to matter /
I desire you to call me yours /

Yet again /

I guess it's easier to accept /
That you are mine /
Than believe I am yours /

For it's easier to accept others /
Than be accepted by others /

Yet again...

You are the calm in the storm /
Your palms never leave me worn /

You are the warmth in the fire /
Constantly pursuing me without tire /

I know deep in my soul /
I have you as my sole...

...Pursuit!, you are my one thing /
God!, this is not a fling /

Cos, I am plastered /
Covered by your presence /

No longer shattered /
You redefine my deepest essence /

No longer feeling battered /
For you are my defence /

No longer flustered /
With you, all thing makes sense /

CLXXXIV

I am not a realist /
Neither do I love idealists /

I have known many people /
Yet they do not know me /

They weren't paying attention /
They weren't listening /

They said I needed community /
Forgetting I was with them all along /

Sometimes I wonder /
Is having community /
Being lonely in the midst of a crowd?
Is it having so many ears around you /
With none of them listening?
Is it having so many voices around you /
With none of them speaking to your heart?
Is it having a long list of numbers /
With none of them actually showing up?

To most /
Being yourself /
Is /
Being like them /

CLXXXV

You are the villain /
Regardless of the lane /
You choose to travel on /
For the good guys /
Are beasts /
In view of the bad guys /

Every battle ends in cries /
As the blood shed dries /
You cannot justify what you are /
For darkness has a lot to say /
When tortured by what light /
Has got to say /

CLXXXVI

What does that even mean /
What should that even be /
Christian dating they call it /
Holy and sacred they paint it /
For a few months /
Boys and girls will be faking it /
Thinking they are making it /
Eros, they will be waking it /
That fire, they will be stoking it /

The time is right so they say /
Let's be together in the bed we lay /
It ends in a fight the next day /
She don't wanna stay /
He's gonna have to pay /
That's the way the world plays /
That's what we mold in clay /

He sat away from me, tiredness in his eyes /
It's been long nights, it's been long years
Yet it felt like yesterday /
He was my friend, I loved him as a brother /
He was in pain, he was stuck /
He had something to say, I had my ears to give /
He said /
"If only I knew what I know about her now /
I wouldn't have been with her" /

Time stopped for me, I was shocked /
I was angry, I was in pain /
I could sense the tunes of regret in his voice /
Yet he braced himself like a man to the challenge /
Because he took a vow when eros was his friend /
Eros is gone, faster than a bullet train /
Betrayed by his own feelings /
By his own perception of what he wanted /

But then I remembered the stories /
How he met her /
How he pursued her /
How he moved mountains to be with her /
How he painted the skies of his love for her...

Oh eros! that desire that paints all things gold /
But then the rain of life comes to wash it all away /
Now I ponder on the words of the ancient /
"Do not awake love until its time" /

Boys and girls can't be friends she said /
Let's walk the path of eros and find Agape /
That's the way it's done /
If we don't find it, let's walk our separate ways /
For it isn't meant to be /

Hearts broken too many times become numb /
Why entrust your heart to those who don't care about theirs /
Life is a gamble they proclaim, love is a risk they project /
Why entrust your future in the hands of those who cast lots with theirs
It takes a lifetime to know a person, I agree /
So why should we be in a hurry I ask /
Why can't we be friends /
Seeking to know a person in the mundane /

Now I ponder on the words of the ancient /
"Do not awaken love until its time" /

Let's be friends /
Yes! let's be friends /
Let's walk the paths of storge /
Developing a familiarity with each other /
Let's take the time to discover phillia /
The connection, that bond us together in friendship /
As we intentionally send eros on exile /
Relegating him to where he belongs, in marriage /
Let's develop an atmosphere where Agape reigns /
for Agape reigns eternal /

They say those who seek friendships /
Are not ready for commitments /
It's funny to me because /
It shows they don't even know where the strongest commitments are formed /
They say those who seek friendships /
Are afraid of being hurt /
It's funny to me because /
They too are scared and don't want to be discovered /

They say those who seek friendships /
Have a different motive /
It's funny to me because /
They're full of broken agendas of the past /
They say those who seek friendships /
Don't know what they want /
It's funny to me because /
They are the most flaky bunch /

Now I ponder on the words of the ancient /
"Do not awake love before its time" /

Words from emotions can't be trusted /
Today it's true, tomorrow something or someone replaces it /
It's either you are or you are not /
Why should anyone take you into their deepest place /
When you haven't shown a glimpse of what you are yet /
Commitment streams from a heart /
Drunk with integrity /
Empty promises flow from a heart /
Drunk with emotions /
Do you do what you say you will do /
Why say it when you can do it /
Actions they say speak louder /
Why entrust your heart to those who keep talking /

CLXXXVII

God won't give you /
What you don't need /
So keep screaming /
"I don't need a man /
I don't need a woman" /
And keep wondering why /
Your bed is only warm /
On certain months /

Not ashamed to say /
I need someone /
It's not a sign of weakness /
But strength and capacity /
Because I know I have a vision /
A legacy to live and share /
And so do they /
We need each other /
Not because of a deficiency /
But for the sake of efficiency /
Neither am I desperate /
Cos I have learnt to grow at my own rate /
However, it's time to spread /

CLXXXVIII

Society says:

"Make up will make you better" /
Yet, your heart is left bitter /
"These clothes will get you attention" /
Yet, your soul is locked in detention /
"You need to have lots of sex" /
Yet, they are vexed - "what a slut /
Can't she keep her legs locked?!" /
"You need to be chaste, why in a haste" /
Yet, they sneer - "what a prude, lacking no taste" /
"You are pretty and confident" - they flatter /
"She's bitchy, it's evident" - they gossip /
Be yourself is preached /
Yet acceptance cannot be reached /

It's an apparition causing apprehension /
A tension causing our souls hypertension /
Self-worth defined by another's imagination /
Self-loathing becomes divination /
Beauty gets botched /
As what is natural gets touched /
"My boobs are too small /
Reason no one's giving me a call" /
"My ass is flat /
Reason no one's giving me a chat" /
You need an enhancement /
Society's argument /

We gulp this poisoning /
Destroying our reasoning /
Ask him what he wants in a woman /
And be shocked at his demand /
Someone who looks like a doll /
Fucks like a mule /
And respects like a fool /
That would be cool /
That is /
He wants the image on the cover /
Of a magazine as a foolish lover /

We are being wired by the superficial /
Constantly choked by the artificial /
Forgetting pictures don't have emotions /
Oh snap! The forgotten omissions /
Let's take an intermission /

Love, 100% commitment, no commission /
A possible indictment without permission /
It's the reality exposing lacks in abilities /
Self-accountability to your own responsibilities /
Yet we hunt for picture perfects /
When reality is full of defects /
He is craving instant gratification /
Causing her constant suffocation /
She becomes a victim of rape /
By a fool who couldn't wait /
Yet she is to blame /
For the boy's inability to quench the flame /
He couldn't have handled /
Now she is entangled /
Forever tied to an image /
A memory causing damage /
Let that seat for a minute /

CLXXXIX

Curiosities becoming deadly weapons /
Alluring mysteries causing mind tickles /
Some things are hiding inside the walls /

Anticipation drowns minds in poisons /
Deciphering where the blood trickles /
Curiosities becoming deadly weapons /

Fears cutting the mind with trepans /
Stealthy harvesting sanity with sickles /
Some things are hiding inside the walls /

Run away, the heart always beckons /
Needs for satisfaction, the mind pickles /
Curiosities becoming deadly weapons /

Entangled in your various deceptions /
molded in sandy reasons with trickles /
Some things are hiding inside the walls /

Mental horrors, our unlearned lessons /
We're deafened to the fear that prickles /
Curiosities becoming deadly weapons /
Some things are hiding inside the walls /

CXC

My identity was rooted in praises /
Betrayals carved it out in phases /
Love didn't give me my deserved wages /
But reasons to bleed in stages /

They said I was crazy /
That my judgements were hazy /
Maybe my mind got lazy /
Have I really been thinking lately?! /

These people be talking behind my back /
Telling the world everything I lacked /
Forgetting when they were shackled /
All those chains I tackled /

Now you free you talking smack /
Through the cracks on your mask /
Pilling up gossips in stacks /
Engaging in silly quacks and attacks /

Yeah... /

I remember that girl named Emily /
Whose actions were so heavenly /
I didn't know she could be an enemy /
Telling the world I committed a felony /

Where the body at, no one is asking /
In falsehood everyone is basking /
You think I don't know what you're masking /
Why do you think I have been laughing /

It is what it is /
This is not a diss /
Just my heart hissing /
What you might be missing /

You can come out of the closet /
You don't like me, I get it /
I'll be truthful and honest /
We ain't friends, now you get it /

CXCI

The little you have is enough /
Don't be scared or worried /
The little he has given you is enough /

Be thankful /
For the little things /

Be hopeful /
For the big things /

Be expectant /
Of everything good in between /

That is how you will travel /
On this journey /

The promises of God are always /
In seed format /
Perhaps it may grow in you /
Because YOU are a carrier of Life /

Water it with your saliva /
Speak it out, make it rain /
Only be ready to harvest it /
That's the only labor /

CXCII

This constant wooing |
That most times ends in booing |
I find myself re-tooling |
Asking who am I fooling |

Layers of my heart peeling |
From the abrasions of torrents of feelings |
The processes of healing |
Becoming by constant dealings |

God, the one I love |
Once again I fall over |
For one who feels like a mover |
I wish this process would roll over |

I don't feel like running after |
Only to realize in her eyes I was a drifter |
Silent whispers of "he is a thrifter" |
He doesn't matter |

But then |
I remember when |
Furious love was after me |
He wouldn't let me be |

I ran so fast |
Yet his expressions were apt |
Blind to my needs of him |
Yet it didn't matter hmmm |

I have immersed myself in books |
Gathering different recipes like a cook |
Researching what love is |
My soul searching for the arena of peace |

Different perspectives cloud my judgements |
My thoughts get entangled in valid arguments |
Argh, I wanna scream |
Thinking it would cool me off like ice-cream |

I need to navigate this path love /
It's who you are, my gentle dove /
I heard from the ancients /
That first, love is patient /
Ah, that blows the fluff away /
Unstable emotions giving way /
Revealing what is true /
Pointing out changes that are due /

But then I remember You
Your constant, persistence, chase after me /
Gentle, never ending, never giving up /
Engraving eternity in my heart /
Love is eternal, never changing /
Even when time changes...
When I look at You? /
Your nature, characteristics never changes /
The same yesterday, today and forever
You God pointp me to what love is /
Now I know where to start making the changes that are due /

CXCIII

10 spies:

They all told the truth /
Skeptics & Critics have great views too /
Keep moving towards the goal /
Knowing they are needed for the fight too /
You will see giants if that's what you are looking for /
You will see milk and honey if that's what you are looking for too /
The truth is every opportunity has potentials for wins and losses /
Question is what are you looking for /

CXCIV

To all the children of light /
Who have given up on God /
Because he didn't do this or that /
Because he hasn't fulfilled this or that /

On behalf of God /
We are sorry /
But please come back home /
Home not defined as "Church" /

Home defined as the secret place /
Where it's just you and him /

It's okay to be mad /
Just come back home /

It's okay to be in that relationship /
Just come back home /

It's okay to have it your way /
Just come back home /

It's okay to feel disappointed /
Just come back home /
It's okay to have waited, trusted, believed, questioned /
Just come back home /

CXCV

When you have tasted fame /
Popular kid on the block /
And suddenly you become unknown /

You begin to appreciate /
The voices that speak to you /
When you feel alone /

The voices that said /
"Am here with you" /
Through all the seasons /
In the highs and lows /

The one that knows you /
And loves you better /
Than anyone can /

CXCVI

Love because you want to /

CXCVII

Sometimes I... /
Intentionally fade away /
Into /
The seen unseen space /
In /
The moments tucked away /
Beneath /
The consciousness of reality /
Cos I am running /
Away from /
Me /

CXCVIII

It's the numbness /
Your love exposed my heart to /
That has become an atmosphere /
Filled with the coldness of many /
Winter nights /

Frozen /
Forgotten /

I am nothing but a reckless savage /
Roaming this jungle called life /
Looking for the next animal to kill /

For food /
For freedom /

CXCIX

When love yearns for devotion /
Without sacrifice! /

We're all too afraid /
To give it all /
To lose it all /

It's not them after all /
But me /
And my inability /
To worship another human being /

For that's the new definition of love /

CC

We need to talk /
Take my hands, lets walk /
Tell me what's on your heart /
Let's create an eternal art /
Give me the fact /
Let's make an impact /
On this love we share /
Let's make a double dare /
Tonight we won't go down /
Until we say those vows /
I want you forever now /
Let's figure out how /

Acknowledgments

We all have dreams. Sometimes what separates us from our dreams are those seasons of battles and uncertainties. It's like traveling through a thick forest, hoping that someday we will get to the other side and discover what we had believed to be ours all along is real.

Most times, we encounter and have to battle wild animals and monsters that prevent us from getting to the other side and sometimes, we will find ourselves on the ground bleeding with eyes blinded by sand or particles of insecurities, pain, bitterness and every negative emotion out there and we just cannot see the hope or the dreams we saw in the distance. Often times, we lie there thinking, accepting everything is over and what we dreamed was nothing but a figment of our own imaginations. We tell ourselves—it was all just a fantasy.

Sometimes, there are seasons where self-help, self-motivation, self-affirmation, self-awareness and everything the self can give to itself is not enough. Sometimes, we find ourselves entangled in the webs of life that are beyond the realms of logic and reasoning.

We realize we are alone, blind, beaten, bleeding.

However, there are fellow travellers in this journey called life who take a detour for you because they see your worth. These people all have goals, dreams, visions and realities they see right in front of them; however, they also see you as being valuable enough by stopping to drag your body to the nearest river, help you wash the dirt off from your eyes and give to you what you cannot give to yourself.

These are the people I call family and friends... These are the people who have stood by me in the last 3 years when I was going through chaos—or should I say depression—that gave birth to this book. I have not directly mentioned or revealed your names because you are all dear to me.

I am thankful to God for giving me parents who are also my best friends. Papa "the great" and Mama J. Thank you for your constant, unending love, encouragement, support and for giving me the gift of identity by introducing me to God and family which gave me the strength to go through the situations that produced this book. Papa, I remember the day you read a poem of mine to Mama. I was a proud young kid and it gave me the strength to keep writing because I saw the joy in your eyes. Thank you Mama J for your constant unending encouragement, your love that defies even gravity. I remember during the moments I wanted to give up on this book, I would always say, "Oh, your Mom is gonna deal with you if you ever give up on anything, so keep going!"

I am thankful to God for my sister "Sister-B". You are my constant encourager, the one who read my original poems when it was still in its most chaotic state and somehow figured it all out. You dragged me to the river and inspired the first half of the title of this book. Your strength and love gives me security. A lot of times people don't understand that the external voices of shame a kid goes through when young becomes the internal voices he fights against when he or she becomes an adult. Thank you for being the constant voice of freedom and self-acceptance that has protected the identity Papa and Mama gave us. You fight for me from a place of love in such a way that I still cannot grasp its depth. You are like that sister who is worth a million brothers put together. With God and you on my side, I can leap over a billion walls.

I am thankful to God for my nephew "Miks". You are my motivation. You call me into greater levels of growth each day. Because of you, I want to be a better man which also inspires me to face my fears... the first being—writing and publishing this book.

I believe it's not the number of friends a man surrounds himself with that makes his life have meaning, but the quality of friends. Thus, I am thankful to God for friends like Swagger-king, Cami, RayRay. You guys helped me pass through the chaotic years that birthed the words within this book and became family to me. When everyone seemed to drift away, you guys remained true, creating an atmosphere of growth in my life's direction of purpose.

To my friend and Aussie cheerleader, "The Purple Queen" who took the time to write my foreword and who, also, kept pushing me forward through the turbulent moments in this journey. Thank you for your time, insight, words of grace and direction. Most importantly, for always checking up on me when I go silent. I remember what you said "If you write an organized book, then I know it's not you". Thanks for being the voice in the world welcoming my raw originality.

To my reviewers comprising of friends, a co-worker and a phenomenal writer and music producer that I adore so much - Pistachio, Bails, Wraith. Thank you so much for taking the time to read my raw draft and providing your honest feedback. I am deeply humbled and honoured. Your words and feedback blew my mind, to be honest.

To the team at Ink Gladiators Press, led by my friend Reena Doss, thank you for taking the time, effort and providing suggestions that has made this book the beauty it is today. If you are an author or aspiring writer—and are reading this—I recommend them for your next project. You won't be disappointed. Why? Empathy is the currency that introduces creativity to the world and these guys are super generous with that.

And last but not least, I acknowledge myself and my alias, Creozoe for allowing God to take my hands in an act of trust to walk and write throughout all the seasons that made this book a possibility. Without God, there is no me.

Author's Note

Dear Readers,

Thank you for taking the time to journey with me through these pages. I truly appreciate it and I hope that my experiences offered either insight into situations or entertained you.

How did this book come to be? I find this question to be interesting as I look back to its start. Writing a book was a dream I had that was buried somewhere within my subconscious. However, I just never thought it was going to be this book.

To simplify the story, I visited a gathering with my friend, Cami where I met her friend Bails who later that day said to me "You remind me of King David in the Bible. You really should write a book". I think those were the first drops of water that provided nourishment to this seed buried deep within my subconscious. From that moment on, I started looking for ideas on what book to write. I remember starting a book titled "Unscrewed". Cami would remember that, but it never lived to see Chapter Two because at that time I had not fully embraced my abilities to communicate through poetry.

Fast forward to 2018-2020, I found myself in situations of hurt, regret, betrayal and all of life's chaos that refines and makes us better human beings. At that time, I was on Instagram where I met my Aussie cheerleader whom I refer to as "The Purple Queen" who was conducting prompt challenges and so I started using them as an inspiration for creativity. I started writing out my pain using these prompts and then she started introducing me to poetry forms which I also took part in. My writing began to grow in a more structured way as I developed expression while adhering to rules (Rules... I ain't no fan of rules!). The poems in here were created during those tough times but there are new ones as well.

I would like to take this opportunity to thank those who caused me pain during those years and those that got close enough for me to hurt because without you all, this book wouldn't have been created. I forgive you and myself.

I wouldn't say the journey in putting this book together was a graceful one, however, if I could turn back the hands of time, I would go through it all over again without editing any part of it because I learned so many things which I will summarize into seven points.

•*If you are talking to everyone, you are talking to no one. You have a voice, find your own audience*
•*Sometimes, to get to the place called "Happy", you have to endure the paths called "SAD".*
•*Depression is an expression about something that you deeply care about but which isn't as important to those who are important to you, not because they don't care, but because you are the one with the power to make beauty out of the ashes of what you care about.*
•*Being Honest, Raw, Original sucks; however, there is no other way.*
•*It's okay to feel awkward. What's not okay is to keep moving backwards for others.*
•*When it comes to relationships, wade through the bullshit and find quality. Unfortunately, the higher the quality you seek, the greater the distance of bullshit you must be willingly to clean up (i.e., your own bullshit).*
•*Be good, not nice, but good.*

That's all I have got to say.

Once again, thank you for picking up my book. Hope it was a blessing in your life. I would love to hear from you. I would love to hear what you think the essence of chaos is about after reading my poems.

Thank you,
Creozoe

Reviews

"The Essence of Chaos is a work of art, a written expression of the divinity that is found in the human experience. The words and poems are drenched in grace and longing to experience wholehearted becoming! It creatively expresses the struggle within the human soul woven together into a singular, yet dynamic breath. What a compelling book of unlearning, and redemption! I cannot wait to buy the hard copy and smell it."
-Bailea Tayler

"Unreserved and experimental, Essence of Chaos reads like the voice in your head. Timi fully embraces his fluctuating emotional state. He captures his inner babblings about love, identity, and pain with a clarity and courage most men would fail to summon for their own diaries. Expect to be pleasantly surprised."
-Trisha Mitra

"Timi, is not just a writer. He is truly an artist. Each piece written here is formed by visions that bounce around inside his soul until they pop out into words on print. This book hits deep with flow that shakes your spirit to the core and ignites passion. After reading it, you will be inspired in so many ways."
-X @a_x_visions_

"Timi always has a way to communicate the language of the soul. He invites the reader to connect with themselves intimately – with their mind, body, soul, and spirit. Timi's writings are like wings that come to cover and heal. This collection of poems clearly displays the cleverness of Timi's use of words, while also offering wisdom that can speak to any situation. Ultimately this book reminds us of our broken humanity, while acknowledging the divine that dwells in us. Timi is a brilliant and discerning writer, he will leave you wanting more."
-Camille Deblois

About The Author

Timi Jolaoso started writing at the age of 7 and identifies himself as an extrovert who does everything in an introverted way. He is a poet, mechanical engineer by profession but also has fun sharpening his designer skills at home. He enjoys having meaningful conversations about things that matter and has the ability to find humour in the ongoing struggles of life. He began writing when he was young to escape the realities of life.

He released his first chapbook "Love Is An Open Door" with co-author Reena Doss last year in May 2020. Timi has also been busy developing his personal brand name and business—Creozoe which means "to create life". His everyday aspiration is to become the best version of himself especially in the little things that make up his whole day. He currently resides in Canada.

Timi Jolaoso has been involved in contributing to a lot of communities in the past. His other manuscripts are in the process of getting edited and finalised but he hopes to publish them as soon as possible. Timi believes that if his books could change a life, it would be the height of literary success to him. He wishes to be a divine inspiration, a catalyst that propels another into becoming their best possible self through the power of words and imagery.

"You have to do what you have to do to be
who you have to be for the sake of yourself and others."

Instagram: creozoe | kingofh_artz | teejols
Spotify Podcast: @kingofh'a:ts | Ticktok: @creozoe | YouTube: @creozoeTV
Email : creozoe@gmail.com
www.creozoe.com | www.creozoe.ca | www.kingofh.art

Please scan the following QR code to follow Timi Jolaoso (Creozoe)

Tell Us What You Think

Write to us at contact@inkgladiatorspress.com and tell us what you think. We appreciate your love for reading.

Thank you!

We remain at your service,
Reena Doss | Founder & CEO
Ink Gladiators Press®

Please scan the following QR code to follow us on Instagram.